Henry Billings
Melissa Billings

New York, New York Columbus, Ohio Chicago, Illinois Peoria, Illinois Woodland Hills, California

JAMESTOWN EDUCATION

The McGraw-Hill Companies

ISBN-13: 978-0-07-874320-7
ISBN-10: 0-07-874320-6

Send all queries to:
Glencoe/McGraw-Hill
8787 Orion Place
Columbus, OH 43240-4027

4 5 6 7 8 9 10 021 10 09

Contents

Unit Three

To the Student

This book has nine articles about celebrities, or famous people, in the world today. Some of the celebrities are movie or television stars. Some are sports players. Others are authors or musicians.

The lives of these stars can inspire us. Some of the stars had tough times while growing up. They worked very hard to find success. Others had to stay focused on their dreams even when other people thought they would fail. And some had to get through challenges even after they became well-known.

In this book you will work on these three specific reading skills:

Asking Questions to Check Comprehension
Fact and Opinion
Drawing Conclusions

You will also work on other reading and vocabulary skills. This will help you understand and think about what you read. The lessons include types of questions often found on state and national tests. Completing the questions can help you get ready for tests you may have to take later.

How to Use This Book

About the Book

This book has three units. Each unit has three lessons. Each lesson has an article about a celebrity followed by practice exercises.

Working Through Each Lesson

Photo Start each lesson by looking at the photo. Read the title and subtitle to get an idea of what the article will focus on.

Think About What You Know, Word Power, Reading Skill This page will help you prepare to read.

Article Now read about the celebrity. Enjoy!

Activities Complete all the activities. Then check your work. Your teacher will give you an answer key to do this. Record the number of your correct answers for each activity. At the end of the lesson, add up your total score for parts A, B, and C. Then find your percentage score in the table. Record your percentage score on the Comprehension and Critical Thinking Progress Graph on page 105.

Compare and Contrast Chart At the end of each unit you will complete a Compare and Contrast Chart. The chart will help you see what some of the celebrities in the unit have in common.

My Personal Dictionary In the back of this book, you can jot down words you would like to know more about. Later you can ask your teacher or a classmate what the words mean. Then you can add the definitions in your own words.

Unit 1

Cuba Gooding Jr.

A Life of Ups and Downs

Birth Name Cuba Gooding Jr.

Birth Date and Place January 2, 1968, The Bronx, New York City

Home Pacific Palisades, California

Think About What You Know

Have you ever been close to something that was a bad influence on you? Were you able to not get involved with it? Read the article to find out how Cuba Gooding Jr. resisted bad influences when he was in school.

Word Power

What do the words below tell you about the article?

limousines large automobiles driven by hired drivers

privileged having a special advantage

siblings someone's brothers or sisters

portrayal the act of playing the part of someone else

typecast to cast an actor repeatedly in the same kind of role

Reading Skill

Asking Questions to Check Comprehension Good readers check their thoughts as they read by stopping and asking themselves questions. Asking questions can help you find out what you do and do not understand. If you can't answer *what, where, when,* or *why* after you read, you can use a fix-up strategy to find the answer. Looking up words you don't understand and asking another student for help are two examples of fix-up strategies.

Example

The movie *Jerry Maguire* is about a man who works as a sports agent. Sports agents represent professional athletes and help the athletes with their careers. An agent might help an athlete get a contract to play on a team. An agent might also help an athlete get work in TV commercials and other types of advertising.

This paragraph talks about sports agents. After reading you might ask yourself, "*What* do sports agents do?" If you don't know the answer, one fix-up strategy might be to go back and reread the paragraph to find the answer. What other fix-up strategies might you use?

Cuba Gooding Jr.

A Life of Ups and Downs

"Show me the money!"

2 If you've seen the movie *Jerry Maguire,* you know that Cuba Gooding Jr.'s character *does* get his money. But even if you've never seen *Jerry Maguire,* you've probably heard someone shout out those words. It's one of the most famous lines ever uttered in a movie, and it helped make Cuba Gooding Jr. a star.

3 In the movie, Gooding Jr.'s character has his ups and downs, but that's nothing compared to the roller coaster ride that Gooding Jr. went through in his own life.

4 Cuba Gooding Jr. was born in 1968 in New York City, where his father began a career as a singer. When Gooding Jr. was three years old, his father joined a band called the Main Ingredient. Over the next few years, this band had several hits, including the wildly popular song "Everybody Plays the Fool." The Goodings seemed guaranteed a wonderful future, and the whole family enjoyed the benefits that came with success. Gooding Jr. rode in **limousines** and hung out backstage with famous performers. When his father performed at Disneyland, officials closed the park and Gooding Jr. got to ride on the merry-go-round with Janet Jackson. Says Gooding Jr., "Until I was 12, I had a pretty **privileged** life."

5 In 1978 the family moved to California, expecting the good times to continue. But two years later, Gooding Jr.'s parents split up, and his dad left the family. Suddenly there wasn't any money for luxuries. There wasn't even enough money for basics. "Things hit rock bottom so quickly it didn't seem real," says Gooding Jr.

6 Gooding Jr.'s mother struggled to find a job that would pay the bills. She became a clerk in a store, often working until midnight, but she still couldn't earn enough to pay the rent. For a while, she and her

children lived in cheap hotels, but soon they couldn't even afford that. "My mother, my **siblings,** and I went from the good life to being homeless," says Gooding Jr. "We lived in a car for a couple of months."

7 Things did not improve much over the next several years. "We moved around a lot," Gooding Jr. recalls. Sometimes the family lived with Gooding Jr.'s grandmother in the Arizona desert. "There was nothing but poverty," says Gooding Jr. "It was rough."

8 Despite all this, Gooding Jr. remained surprisingly hopeful. He dreamed of becoming a star—and he vowed not to let poverty ruin his dream. All around him, people were turning to guns and drugs, but he knew he didn't want that kind of a life. "I hung out with a lot of guys who ran in gangs," he says, "but I never was a member of one."

9 Instead, Gooding Jr. focused on other activities. He took any job he could find. He weeded people's gardens and sold tacos at a taco stand. He worked as a clerk in a mall. He also got a job as a telemarketer, trying to sell people products over the telephone.

10 Having those jobs meant some very long days for Gooding Jr. "At one point in my life, I was getting on a bus at 6:00 in the morning, at school by 7:30, doing my homework for about 45 minutes before school started, and going until 3:00. I did a couple more hours of homework on the bus going to work, and then I worked from 5:00 to 11:00," says Gooding Jr. He took the bus back home, and it was often 1:00 in the morning before he got to bed. "I did this all week long," he says.

Skill Break

Asking Questions to Check Comprehension

Look at paragraph 10 on this page. The paragraph tells about Gooding Jr.'s busy schedule as a student.

What **question** can you ask yourself to check your understanding of what Gooding Jr.'s day was like?

What **fix-up strategy** might you use if you had trouble answering your question?

11 Because his family moved so frequently, Gooding Jr. went to four different high schools. Yet at each new school, he managed to do well. At three of his four schools he was elected class president!

12 Gooding Jr. got his first taste of show business in 1984, when he was chosen to be a break dancer at the closing ceremonies of the 1984 Olympics. Soon after that, he performed in a high school play. A parent in the audience happened to be a Hollywood agent. The agent was impressed with Gooding Jr.'s performance and offered to help him get acting jobs.

13 Over the next few years, Gooding Jr. landed several small roles in TV shows and appeared in a couple of commercials. But his first big success came in 1991, with *Boyz N the Hood.* In this movie, Gooding Jr. proved that he was an actor to be taken seriously. His **portrayal** of a young man trying to get out of South Central Los Angeles impressed many people.

14 After *Boyz N the Hood,* Gooding Jr. hoped a wide variety of roles would come his way. "I wanted to be a cowboy, I wanted to be a pirate, I wanted to be a businessman," he says. Hollywood didn't have that many good roles for African American actors, however, and Gooding Jr. found himself looking at more roles like the one he played in *Boyz.* He says, "The scripts I got were *Boyz N the Hood 2 . . . Boyz N the Hood Goes to Heaven, Boyz N the Hood Goes to the Laundromat, Boyz at the Supermarket."* Gooding Jr. didn't want to be **typecast** as a gang member, so he rejected all these roles.

- Gooding Jr. likes to play ice hockey.
- He has a roller-hockey rink in his home.
- He has studied Japanese martial arts.
- He almost didn't get the part of Rod Tidwell because he was considered too short.

Gooding Jr.'s character, Rod Tidwell, gets angry in this scene from the movie *Jerry Maguire.*

15 In 1996 he finally saw his chance. Gooding Jr. wanted to play Rod Tidwell, the football player in *Jerry Maguire* whose favorite expression is "Show me the money!" He auditioned and convinced the director to hire him. It was a good decision: Gooding Jr. turned in an Oscar-winning performance.

16 After *Jerry Maguire,* Gooding Jr. starred in many other movies, including *Pearl Harbor* (2001) and *Radio* (2003). Today he is one of the biggest stars in Hollywood. Yet he remains the cheerful, friendly person he has always been. Gooding Jr. knows from experience that success doesn't always last, so he has put much of his energy into building a good life beyond the big screen. He has been married to his high-school sweetheart since 1994, and they have two sons, Spencer and Mason.

17 Gooding Jr. is grateful for his family, his health, and his current good fortune. He is thankful for all that he has—and he tries to squeeze all the happiness he can out of each day. As he says, "Every day above ground is a good one, man."

A Understanding What You Read

◆ **Fill in the circle next to the correct answer.**

1. What was the effect on Gooding Jr.'s family when his dad left?

○ A. The Goodings had to cancel their trip to Disneyland.
○ B. The Goodings didn't have enough money for basics.
○ C. The Goodings weren't able to stay in Arizona.

2. How did Gooding Jr. first start getting acting jobs?

○ A. A Hollywood agent offered to help him.
○ B. Someone saw him dance at the Olympics.
○ C. A director gave him a part in a movie.

3. Gooding Jr. won an award for his performance in

○ A. *Boyz N the Hood.*
○ B. *Jerry Maguire.*
○ C. *Pearl Harbor.*

4. Which of the following statements is an opinion rather than a fact?

○ A. The family moved to California in 1978.
○ B. He also got a job as a telemarketer.
○ C. Every day above ground is a good one.

5. Which sentence **best** states the lesson about life that this article teaches?

○ A. Be grateful for all that you have.
○ B. It's important to repay your debts.
○ C. Don't take your goals too seriously.

_____ Number of Correct Answers: Part A

B Asking Questions to Check Comprehension

◆ **Read the paragraphs below. Fill in the circle next to the question that would best help you check your understanding of the article.**

1.

In 1978 the family moved to California, expecting the good times to continue. But two years later, Gooding Jr.'s parents split up, and his dad left the family. Suddenly there wasn't any money for luxuries. There wasn't even enough money for basics. "Things hit rock bottom so quickly it didn't seem real," says Gooding Jr.

Gooding Jr.'s mother struggled to find a job that would pay the bills. She became a clerk in a store, often working until midnight, but she still couldn't earn enough to pay the rent. For a while, she and her children lived in cheap hotels, but soon they couldn't even afford that. "My mother, my siblings, and I went from the good life to being homeless," says Gooding Jr. "We lived in a car for a couple of months."

○ A. What kind of car did the Goodings have?
○ B. Where was the hotel where the Goodings stayed?
○ C. Why did the Goodings become homeless?

◆ **Suppose you couldn't answer the question you selected above. Write two fix-up strategies you might use to find the answer.**

2. ______________________________

____

____

____

______ Number of Correct Answers: Part B

C Using Words

◆ **Complete the analogies below by writing a word from the box on each line. Remember that in an analogy, the last two words or phrases must be related in the same way that the first two are related.**

limousines	**siblings**	**typecast**
privileged	**portrayal**	

1. father : parents :: brother : ________________

2. quick : speedy :: special : ________________

3. scientist : classify :: director : ________________

4. pilots : airplanes :: drivers : ________________

5. artist : painting :: actor : ________________

◆ **Choose one word from the box. Write a sentence using the word.**

6. word: ________________

____

____

______ Number of Correct Answers: Part C

D Writing About It

Write Interview Questions

◆ Suppose you have a chance to interview Cuba Gooding Jr. Write **four** questions you would like to ask. Use the checklist on page 103 to check your work.

1. ____

____

2. ____

____

3. ____

____

4. ____

____

Lesson 1 Add your correct answers from parts A, B, and C to get your total score. Then find the percentage for your total score on the chart below. Record your percentage on the graph on page 105.

______ Total Score for Parts A, B, and C

______ Percentage

Total Score	1	2	3	4	5	6	7	8	9	10	11	12	13
Percentage	8	15	23	31	38	46	54	62	69	77	85	92	100

Shakira

Believing in Herself

Birth Name Shakira Isabel Mebarak Ripoll

Birth Date and Place February 2, 1977, Barranquilla, Colombia

Home Miami, Florida

Think About What You Know

Do you know what type of career you want to have when you get older? How certain are you about what you want? Read the article to find out how certain Shakira was about her childhood dream.

Word Power

What do the words below tell you about the article?

prophecy something that was told or predicted beforehand

bankrupt unable to pay off debts

executive a manager who leads a company or business

refined improved upon by removing weaknesses and adding finishing details

mainstream following the most popular direction, activity, or interest

Reading Skill

Fact and Opinion A **fact** is a statement that can be proved. A fact can be checked using a reference source. An **opinion** is someone's own idea about something. The text may include clue words that show statements of opinion. Words such as *I think, in her opinion,* and *he believes* show statements of opinion.

Example

Fact Throughout the world people speak many different languages, including English, Spanish, and Italian.

Opinion I think it is easy to learn a new language.

The statement "Throughout the world people speak many different languages, including English, Spanish, and Italian" is true and can be proved. It is a fact. The statement "I think it is easy to learn a new language" is what someone thinks. It is an opinion. What clue words in the second statement help show the reader that it is an opinion?

Shakira

Believing in Herself

Some children have no idea what they want to be when they grow up. But that was not the case with Shakira. "You can laugh," she says, "but since I was a child I knew that I was going to be a well-known singer and songwriter. That was something I had no doubts about. It was almost like a **prophecy.** It was like an appointment I was getting ready for and I had to meet."

2 Shakira caught a glimpse of her destiny at the age of four, when she first performed in public. Shakira, whose mother is Colombian and whose father is Lebanese, performed a Middle Eastern belly dance at her preschool. She loved being on stage and hearing people applaud for her, and she knew then that she wanted to be a performer. By the age of eight, she had started writing her own songs.

3 During these early years, Shakira led a very comfortable life. Her parents owned several jewelry stores in Colombia and had plenty of money to spend. That changed, however, when Shakira was nine years old. The jewelry stores went **bankrupt,** a development that caused the family to make many adjustments. "We had to sell both cars, and the big television became a black-and-white television," she recalls. "The big bed became a regular bed. It was, somehow, a big change."

4 Shakira's parents wanted their daughter to know that she was still very fortunate, though, so they made a point of showing her what true poverty was. "They took me to a park where all the homeless children are, and they showed me that sad side of life," she recalls. "It was really a tragedy to know that these children didn't have parents to take care of them."

5 Shakira got the message, and she didn't complain about her family's reduced circumstances. Instead she stayed focused on her goal of becoming a successful performer. She listened to all sorts of music, from rock 'n' roll to Arabic songs to Latin ballads. She learned to play the guitar and the harmonica, and she imagined herself becoming a rock 'n' roll star, a supermodel, an actress, a belly dancer, a pop singer—or all of the above! Whatever her future held, she believed she had the talent to become famous.

6 Not everyone shared that belief. Shakira's elementary school music teacher certainly didn't. He didn't like Shakira's voice. He thought it sounded like "the bleating of a goat." He even asked her not to sing in the school choir because he believed she would throw everyone else off-key. Some people would have been discouraged by this criticism—but not Shakira. She simply decided to pursue music outside of school. She found some local singing contests to enter, and by the age of 11 she began winning both local and national prizes.

7 When Shakira was 13, she had written enough songs to put together an album. She made her way to a record studio in Bogotá, Colombia, where she caught the attention of a studio **executive** by singing in his office lobby. He signed her to a contract, and the following year her first album came out. It was called *Magia,* which is Spanish for "magic."

Skill Break

Fact and Opinion

Look at paragraph 5 on this page. The paragraph describes what Shakira did to prepare herself for a career as a performer.

What statement in the paragraph shows someone's **opinion?**

What **clue words** did you use?

8 Over the next few years, Shakira **refined** her talent, adding more rock to her Latin pop sound. She finished high school and began acting in a Colombian soap opera, but she soon returned to her music. Her album *Pies descalzos (Bare Feet)* came out in 1995, eventually topping the charts in eight countries.

9 By the age of 21, Shakira was a huge star in most Spanish-speaking countries. For many people this would have been enough, but Shakira wanted more. She wanted to become well known in the United States. To do that, she turned to Emilio and Gloria Estefan, a Cuban American couple who had become leaders in the American music industry. She hired Emilio to become her manager and producer of her next album, *¿Dónde están los ladrones? (Where Are the Thieves?).*

10 This third album was an even bigger hit than her previous two. Several of the songs made it to the top of the U.S. Latin Billboard chart, and by the end of the year Shakira had won two Latin Grammy Awards. But she and the Estefans agreed that she had to begin singing in English. They thought it was the only way to reach the **mainstream** audience in the United States.

11 Gloria Estefan offered to take some of Shakira's Spanish songs and translate them into English for her, but Shakira didn't want to do that. "I needed to write new songs," she says. "I was in a place in my life where I had many new things to tell. I wanted to explore new sounds. It was best for me to start from zero, not translate into English songs that have been sitting around from before." Shakira could have

- Shakira speaks five languages.
- She started a foundation that provides shoes to needy children.
- Her name means "full of grace" in Arabic.

Shakira, whose hair is naturally brown, dyed her hair blonde before her album *Laundry Service* was released.

written new songs in Spanish and asked Gloria to translate those, but she didn't want to do that either. She wanted to choose exactly which words were used. She believed that the only way for her to do that was write the songs herself—in English.

12 For the next year and a half, Shakira worked hard studying English. She spent months perfecting the phrasing of each new song. "I had to find a way to express my ideas and my feelings, my day-to-day stories in English," she says. "So I bought a couple of rhyming dictionaries, and read poetry and authors like Leonard Cohen and Walt Whitman." At last she felt ready to turn her work over to the studio executives. "I didn't know what the reaction was going to be," she says. She needn't have worried. Everyone loved her new work, which was put together into the album *Laundry Service*. One of the songs, "Whenever/ Wherever," was made into a music video, helping to make Shakira a superstar in the United States almost overnight.

13 At the age of 24, Shakira had done it. She had become a world-wide celebrity, wildly popular in Spanish-speaking countries and with many fans in the United States as well. Shakira had been right all along. Her talent—and her belief in that talent—had made her a star.

A Understanding What You Read

◆ **Fill in the circle next to the correct answer.**

1. When Shakira performed in preschool,

○ A. she sang a song that she had written herself.

○ B. she loved hearing people applaud for her.

○ C. her voice sounded like the call of a goat.

2. An executive at a record studio offered Shakira a recording contract when she

○ A. sang in the office lobby.

○ B. performed as a belly dancer.

○ C. appeared on a soap opera.

3. From the information in the article, you can predict that

○ A. fans will want to buy more Shakira albums.

○ B. more Colombian singers will become big stars.

○ C. Shakira will appear in a new soap opera.

4. The author probably wrote this article in order to

○ A. persuade the reader to see Shakira perform.

○ B. entertain the reader with a wild story about Shakira.

○ C. inform the reader about Shakira's life and her career.

5. Which of the following categories would this article fit into?

○ A. Best Latin Albums of the Year

○ B. People Who Follow Their Dreams

○ C. New Hollywood Movie Stars

_____ Number of Correct Answers: Part A

B Understanding Fact and Opinion

◆ **Read the paragraph below. Write the letter *O* on the lines next to statements that show someone's opinion. Write the letter *F* on the lines next to statements that are facts.**

1.

Not everyone shared that belief. Shakira's elementary school music teacher certainly didn't. He didn't like Shakira's voice. He thought it sounded like "the bleating of a goat." He even asked her not to sing in the school choir because he believed she would throw everyone else off-key. Some people would have been discouraged by this criticism—but not Shakira. She simply decided to pursue music outside of school. She found some local singing contests to enter, and by the age of 11 she began winning both local and national prizes.

_______ He thought it sounded like "the bleating of a goat."

_______ He asked her not to sing in the school choir.

_______ He believed she would throw everyone else off-key.

_______ She began winning both local and national prizes.

◆ **Reread paragraph 10 from the article. Write one statement from the paragraph that shows someone's opinion. Then write the clue words you used.**

2. Opinion: ____

Clue words: ____

_______ Number of Correct Answers: Part B

C Using Words

◆ Cross out one of the four words in each row that does **not** relate to the word in dark type.

1. prophecy

future	defense	event	forecast

2. bankrupt

broke	finance	owe	ripe

3. executive

nursery	leader	decisions	responsible

4. refined

smooth	better	wired	clean

5. mainstream

usual	many	popular	pointed

◆ Choose one of the words shown in dark type above. Write a sentence using the word.

6. word: ____________________

____

____

_____ Number of Correct Answers: Part C

D Writing About It

Write a Book Cover

◆ Write an advertisement for Shakira's album *Laundry Service.* Include information about Shakira's music and how she came to make this album. Write at least four sentences. Use the checklist on page 103 to check your work.

Now Available

Laundry Service, by Shakira

Now Available

____

____

____

____

____

____

Lesson 2 Add your correct answers from parts A, B, and C to get your total score. Then find the percentage for your total score on the chart below. Record your percentage on the graph on page 105.

_____ Total Score for Parts A, B, and C

_____ Percentage

Total Score	1	2	3	4	5	6	7	8	9	10	11	12	13
Percentage	8	15	23	31	38	46	54	62	69	77	85	92	100

Tavis Smiley

Keeping the Faith

Birth Name Tavis Smiley

Birth Date and Place September 13, 1964, Gulfport, Mississippi

Home Los Angeles, California

Think About What You Know

Have you ever wanted to speak out for something you believe in? Read the article to find out how Tavis Smiley became a leader who speaks up for what he believes in.

Word Power

What do the words below tell you about the article?

obnoxious extremely annoying and unpleasant

celebrity someone who is well-known or famous

advocates people who publicly support a cause

devalue to lessen the worth or importance of something

prosperity a state of wealth or success

Reading Skill

Drawing Conclusions Good readers **draw conclusions.** They combine information from several parts of an article with what they already know to find a bigger idea. As you read, look for details that provide clues about the people and events in the article. Then, when you draw a conclusion, make sure it is supported by at least two clues in the text.

Example

Radio is a part of many people's daily lives. People can listen to the radio at home, at work, and in their cars. Some people even carry radios with them. There are a wide variety of music, news, and talk stations for people to choose from.

What do you already know about radio? One thing you might know is that *many people like to listen to the radio.* So a conclusion that you might draw from this paragraph is that *radio is a useful tool for communicating with many people.* What are two clues from the paragraph that support this conclusion?

Tavis Smiley

Keeping the Faith

"I have discovered that if you act like a normal human being, you'll be treated like a normal human being."

2 That is Tavis Smiley's explanation for why he won't ride in limousines. Smiley considers limousines to be loud and **obnoxious,** and he doesn't like the way they attract attention. "I have found that when you act like a **celebrity,** people treat you like one," he says. Although Smiley is one of the most famous radio and television talk show hosts in the United States, he doesn't want special treatment. He works to maintain a style of life as he's "always lived it."

3 For Smiley, that style of life is pretty simple. He grew up in Kokomo, Indiana, in humble surroundings. The third of ten children, he lived with his family in a three-bedroom mobile home and shared a bedroom with his six brothers. His mother worked as a minister, and his father, a master sergeant in the Air Force, worked a variety of extra jobs to bring in money. "We never had a lot of what we wanted," he says, "but I can't say we ever went hungry either." The family had so little money, though, that Smiley used cardboard to cover the holes in his shoes.

4 As a young boy, Smiley dreamed of becoming a baseball player, but at age 13 his dreams changed. He developed an admiration for Douglas Hogan, a city council member who did everything from getting potholes filled to getting teenagers summer jobs. Smiley began to think that he would like to help people too. Then one night Smiley heard a campaign speech given by U.S. Senator Birch Bayh. Smiley realized how much power politicians have to help people. "That night I gave up my dreams of being a first baseman in the major leagues," he recalls. "I decided I wanted to devote my life to public service."

5 Over the next few years, Smiley developed his skills as a leader. In his nearly all-white high school, his classmates elected him class president as a junior and again as a senior. They made him captain of the debate team and voted him "most likely to succeed."

6 After high school, Smiley entered Indiana University. During his sophomore year there, the police shot and killed one of his friends. Although the police said they had been defending themselves, Smiley believed that the police officers, who were white, had killed his African American friend on purpose. That's when Smiley realized that he didn't want to enter politics "just to get potholes fixed and trees trimmed and get kids summer jobs—but also to right wrongs."

7 Smiley moved to California after finishing college. He went to work for Tom Bradley, the first African American mayor of Los Angeles. Then at the age of 26, Smiley ran for political office, campaigning for a seat on the city council. He lost. Smiley knew one reason he lost was that voters didn't know him. To build up his name recognition for a second try, Smiley began doing 60-second talks on KGFJ, an African American radio station. He called it *The Smiley Report.* Other radio stations began to broadcast the show. Soon Smiley had his own talk show on Black Entertainment Television (BET). The show, called *BET Tonight with Tavis Smiley,* launched him in a different direction, and he never ran for public office again. Smiley had found a new career.

Skill Break

Drawing Conclusions

Look at paragraph 5 on this page. The paragraph describes some of the things that happened when Smiley was in high school. One **conclusion** the reader might draw from this paragraph is that *Smiley had natural leadership skills that influenced his classmates.*

How do the **clues** in the paragraph support this conclusion?

How does **what you already know** support this conclusion?

8 In recent years, Smiley has hosted a variety of TV and radio talk shows, including one for the Public Broadcasting System (PBS) and one for National Public Radio (NPR). He loves this work because, as he puts it, "it's a high-profile job that allows you to say whatever you want—and keep in constant contact with the public." Smiley has indeed reached millions of people with his shows. In 1999 *Newsweek* magazine called him one of the nation's "captains of the airwaves" and claimed that he is one of the "20 people changing how Americans get their news."

9 But Smiley isn't interested in just telling people the news. He wants them to act. "What I tell black people every day on the radio is to be **advocates,**" he says. To make a difference, he adds, "You've got to fight for these things you believe in." Over the years Smiley has used his voice to create change. For example, he has gotten businesses to direct more of their advertising spots to African American-owned radio stations. Again and again Smiley has spoken out about what he feels is wrong in the United States. He wants other people, especially African Americans, to raise their voices too. He says they need to get in the habit of "writing and calling and faxing and e-mailing" their opinions to leaders. "Politics," declares Smiley, "is not a spectator sport."

10 Smiley has also reached his audience through books. He has written more than half a dozen books, including the best-seller *Keeping the Faith: Stories of Love, Courage, Healing and Hope from Black America.*

- Smiley enjoys playing word games.
- He played an important role in getting Rosa Parks awarded the Presidential Medal of Freedom.
- His childhood heroes were Malcom X and Dr. Martin Luther King Jr.
- He likes any food besides liver and onions.

Tavis Smiley speaks about the opening of the Tavis Smiley Center for Professional Media Studies at a 2004 press conference in Houston, Texas.

In addition he has established the Tavis Smiley Foundation. Its goal is to help African American children by offering scholarships and programs in leadership.

11 Smiley knows he can't solve all the world's problems. But he believes there is honor in fighting for what is right, even if you don't always win. "Life, by definition, is a series of ups and downs," he says. "The bad news is that you won't always be up, but the good news is that you won't always be down either." Through all the ups and downs, the important thing, he says, is "to keep the faith."

12 Smiley's message appeals to people, and he has a great deal of popular support, especially in the African American community. Someone once asked him why so many African Americans like him. His response was that it is a matter of trust. As his attitude about limousines suggests, Tavis Smiley is no phony. What you see and hear is real. "At the end of the day I am a black man," he says. "I love being black and love black people. And I will never, ever **devalue** or take for granted the trust of black people."

13 His father, Emory Smiley, phrases it this way. "One main thing that I have really admired about Tavis," says Mr. Smiley, "is that through all of his fame and **prosperity,** he has not forgotten his roots."

A Understanding What You Read

◆ **Fill in the circle next to the correct answer.**

1. Smiley gave up his dream of becoming a baseball player because he

○ A. wanted to devote his life to serving the public.
○ B. realized he wasn't a very good baseball player.
○ C. needed to earn money to help his family.

2. Which of the following statements is an opinion rather than a fact?

○ A. One of his goals is to help African American children.
○ B. You've got to fight for these things you believe in.
○ C. Smiley used cardboard to cover the holes in his shoes.

3. Smiley began doing 60-second radio talks so he could

○ A. support Black Entertainment Television.
○ B. begin hosting his own radio talk show.
○ C. build up his name recognition.

4. From the information in the article, you can predict that

○ A. more celebrities will stop riding in limousines.
○ B. the Tavis Smiley Foundation will help many children.
○ C. Smiley will soon decide to run for public office again.

5. Which sentence **best** states the main idea of the article?

○ A. Smiley wants people to fight for the things they believe in.
○ B. Smiley reaches millions of people with his shows.
○ C. Smiley is a talk show host who speaks out to right wrongs.

_____ Number of Correct Answers: Part A

B Drawing Conclusions

◆ **Read the paragraph below. Fill in the circle next to the conclusion that is best supported by the information in the paragraph.**

1.

As a young boy, Smiley dreamed of becoming a baseball player, but at age 13 his dreams changed. He developed an admiration for Douglas Hogan, a city council member who did everything from getting potholes filled to getting teenagers summer jobs. Smiley began to think that he would like to help people too. Then one night Smiley heard a campaign speech given by U.S. Senator Birch Bayh. Smiley realized how much power politicians have to help people. "That night I gave up my dreams of being a first baseman in the major leagues," he recalls. "I decided I wanted to devote my life to public service."

○ A. Smiley is a thoughtful and caring person.
○ B. Smiley will do whatever it takes to be successful.
○ C. Smiley thought carefully before giving up his baseball dream.

◆ **What clues from the paragraph support this conclusion? Write two clues. Then explain how what you already know helped you draw this conclusion.**

2. Clue: ______________________________

Clue: ______________________________

What I Know: ______________________________

____

______ Number of Correct Answers: Part B

C Using Words

◆ The words and phrases in the list below relate to the words in the box. Some words or phrases in the list have a meaning that is the same as or similar to a word in the box. Some have the opposite meaning. Write the related word from the box on each line. Use each word from the box twice.

obnoxious	advocates	prosperity
celebrity	devalue	

Same or similar meaning

1. superstar ________________
2. to lower ________________
3. good fortune ________________
4. believers ________________
5. awful ________________

Opposite meaning

6. opponents ________________
7. unknown ________________
8. appealing ________________
9. regard highly ________________
10. poverty ________________

_____ Number of Correct Answers: Part C

D Writing About It

Write a Speech

◆ Write a speech about Tavis Smiley's career and what he believes is important. Write at least four sentences. Use the checklist on page 103 to check your work.

____

____

____

____

____

____

____

____

____

____

Lesson 3 Add your correct answers from parts A, B, and C to get your total score. Then find the percentage for your total score on the chart below. Record your percentage on the graph on page 105.

_____ Total Score for Parts A, B, and C

_____ Percentage

Total Score	1	2	3	4	5	6	7	8	9	10	11	12	13	14	15	16	17
Percentage	6	12	18	24	29	35	41	47	53	59	65	70	76	82	88	94	100

Compare and Contrast

◆ Think about the celebrities, or famous people, in Unit One. Pick two articles that tell about celebrities who have a strong belief about something. Use information from the articles to fill in this chart.

Celebrity's Name		
What does the celebrity believe?		
What experiences helped form this belief?		
What actions has the celebrity taken as a result of this belief?		

Unit 2

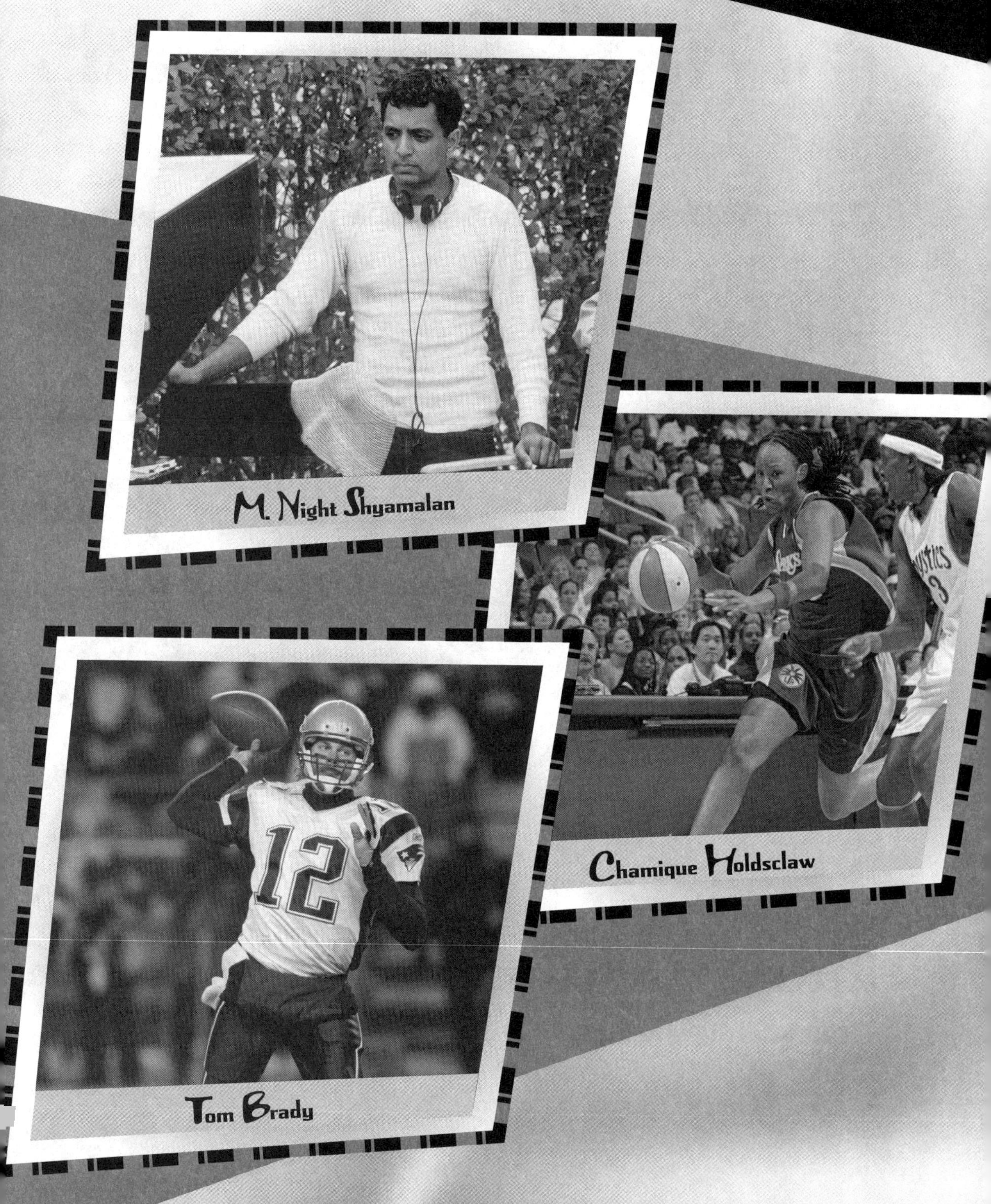

M. Night Shyamalan

Man of Mystery

Birth Name Manoj Nelliyattu Shyamalan

Birth Date and Place August 6, 1970, Pondicherry, Tamil-Nadu, India

Home Wayne, Pennsylvania

Think About What You Know

Do you enjoy watching scary movies? Have you ever thought about making a movie yourself? Read the article to find out how M. Night Shyamalan became a successful movie director.

Word Power

What do the words below tell you about the article?

mangle to do something imperfectly or to mess something up

psychologist someone who is trained in the study of the mind, emotions, and behavior

unveiling opening to view by taking away a covering

inaction stillness or lack of movement

unconventional out of the ordinary

Reading Skill

Asking Questions to Check Comprehension Good readers check their understanding as they read. They use fix-up strategies that help them get back on track when their understanding breaks down. As you read, stop and ask yourself questions about the text. When you can't answer a question, think about what you might do as a fix-up strategy. One fix-up strategy is to reread the text. Another is to look up any unknown words.

Example

These days, more and more kids are finding opportunities to make their own movies. Many schools and families own digital video cameras, and it's easier than ever to edit movies on a computer. Some computer programs even let you add captions, special effects, and music to your movies.

While reading this paragraph, you might ask yourself, "Why are more kids making their own movies?" One fix-up strategy you can use if you can't answer this question is to ask someone who makes home movies to explain why they do it. What other fix-up strategies could you use?

M. Night Shyamalan

Man of Mystery

His films are spooky and unpredictable. They're full of eerie situations and unexplainable events. And don't be surprised if there's a ghost or an alien thrown in for good measure.

2 Welcome to the world of M. Night Shyamalan, one of the hottest movie directors in Hollywood. In a 2002 cover story, *Newsweek* magazine wondered if Shyamalan might be the next Steven Spielberg, the famous director of such all-time movie favorites as *Jaws, E.T., Jurassic Park,* and the Indiana Jones series. Shyamalan is in such demand that he is one of the few directors who can "sell" a movie just with his name. Millions of people will rush to see a Tom Cruise movie just because he's in it. In the same way, millions will go see a Shyamalan movie knowing nothing more than that he made it.

3 It certainly wasn't his parents' dream that Manoj Nelliyattu Shyamalan would grow up to be a movie director. His mother and father are both doctors, and there are 14 doctors in the extended Shyamalan family. So his parents naturally imagined that their son might become a doctor too. But their hopes were doomed the day eight-year-old Shyamalan got a Super-8 movie camera. He fell in love with filmmaking, putting together 45 home movies over the next 10 years.

4 In 1988 Shyamalan entered New York University's Tisch School of the Arts to study film. While in college, he decided to change his name. He abbreviated his first name to the initial *M.* Manoj was simply too hard to pronounce, and he was tired of hearing his teachers **mangle** it. In addition, he dropped his middle name and took on the more memorable Night. According to his father, he chose that name in part because of his interest in the Native American ritual of telling stories around a campfire at night and in part because it's only at night that a person can look out at the stars and glimpse

the greater universe. There was a practical consideration as well. As Shyamalan's father puts it, Night is "a good entertainment name."

5 Shyamalan graduated from NYU in 1992, the same year he produced his first film. It was titled *Praying with Anger* and was based in part on a trip he made back to India, the country where he was born. Six years later he made his second film, *Wide Awake*. Neither of these films were popular with audiences or critics.

6 Shyamalan was disappointed but not discouraged. "I decided I was going to write the greatest script, and everything was going to change," he says. So he sat down and began to write. His first draft wasn't very good, and his second draft wasn't much better. "It wasn't until about the fifth draft that I really began to figure it out," he says. Slowly, the story he wanted to tell began to appear. Still, it took him five more rewrites before he got it right.

7 The result of all this writing and rewriting was *The Sixth Sense,* an intriguing thriller starring Bruce Willis as a **psychologist** and 10-year-old Haley Joel Osment as a boy who can see and talk to people who have died. The movie, with its gripping storyline and shocking conclusion, caught everyone in Hollywood by surprise. No one expected it to be particularly successful. But *The Sixth Sense* connected with audiences in a special way. People who saw it told their friends about it, and this word-of-mouth advertising soon made it one of the biggest hits ever. The film earned nearly $700 million and picked up six Oscar nominations, including for Best Director and Best Original Screenplay.

Skill Break

Asking Questions to Check Comprehension

Look at paragraph 7 on this page. The paragraph describes what happened after Shyamalan made the movie *The Sixth Sense.*

What **question** can you ask to help check your understanding of the movie's big success?

What **fix-up strategy** could you use to help you answer your question?

8 Suddenly Shyamalan was hot. People could hardly wait to see what he would do next. His next movie was *Unbreakable,* which also stars Bruce Willis. This time Willis plays a security guard who has mysterious powers—or at least that's how it seems when he walks away from a train wreck that kills everyone on board but leaves him completely unharmed. Like *The Sixth Sense,* this movie slowly builds tension and finishes with a surprise ending.

9 After that Shyamalan wrote and directed *Signs,* a movie starring Mel Gibson as the head of a farm family scared by the sudden appearance of crop circles in their cornfield. Did aliens make these circles as a guide for their spaceships? As with Shyamalan's other movies, this film spooks the audience with silence and the slow, careful **unveiling** of information. As movie reviewer Roger Ebert writes, "I cannot think of a movie where silence is scarier, and **inaction** is more disturbing."

10 Shyamalan's next film, *The Village,* was released in 2004. It tells of a late-nineteenth-century village isolated from the world and threatened by an evil force lying just beyond the town boundaries. Once again, Shyamalan offers plenty of suspense, interesting characters, and a shocking twist at the end.

Fun Facts

- Shyamalan loves reading comic books.
- He wears a silver charm around his neck given to him by his father.
- In his movies, the color red often indicates an important clue.
- He makes a brief appearance on screen in all his movies.

M. Night Shyamalan works on the set of the popular thriller *Signs*.

11 Because Shyamalan's movies so often have unexpected endings, he has to work to keep the element of surprise intact. He knows it might ruin the movie experience if people know at the beginning how the film ends. Luckily, most movie reviewers don't give away his endings, and neither do most movie-goers. But Shyamalan still treats his stories as if they were military secrets. Adrien Brody, who stars in *The Village,* said, "My agents weren't even allowed to read the script." His co-star, Sigourney Weaver, said, "I felt like I was part of a secret society."

12 Joaquin Phoenix, who also stars in *The Village,* thinks this is a good thing. Says Phoenix, "I wish all films were like that. I can't stand when directors and actors talk about what a movie is about or their characters. I want to discover that for myself. To me that's the whole point."

13 By now people have come to expect **unconventional** things from M. Night Shyamalan. And that's the way he likes it. He intends to go on making films that thrill audiences but also cause them to walk away thinking about what they have seen. So if you ever find yourself sitting in a theater and you see the name Shyamalan flash across the screen, be prepared. You'll know that the next hours will take you on a wild—and probably very scary—journey.

A Understanding What You Read

◆ **Fill in the circle next to the correct answer for numbers 1, 2, 3, and 5. Follow the directions shown for number 4.**

1. Shyamalan's parents once thought he would become a

○ A. writer.

○ B. doctor.

○ C. entertainer.

2. From what you read in the article, M. Night Shyamalan and Steven Spielberg are alike because both

○ A. like to have Tom Cruise star in their movies.

○ B. have worked on the Indiana Jones movies.

○ C. have directed movies that became big hits.

3. Shyamalan rewrote the script for *The Sixth Sense* many times because

○ A. it took him a while to figure out how to tell the story.

○ B. people in Hollywood didn't think it was a good story.

○ C. he was busy finishing his film degree at NYU.

4. In which paragraph did you find the information to answer question 3?

______

5. From what you read in the article, which of these is probably true?

○ A. The movie *The Village* is based on a Native American ritual.

○ B. The movie *Signs* has a surprising conclusion.

○ C. The movie *Wide Awake* received an Oscar nomination.

______ Number of Correct Answers: Part A

B Asking Questions to Check Comprehension

◆ **Read the paragraph below. Fill in the circle next to the question that would best help you check your understanding of the article.**

1.

In 1988 Shyamalan entered New York University's Tisch School of the Arts to study film. While in college, he decided to change his name. He abbreviated his first name to the initial *M.* Manoj was simply too hard to pronounce, and he was tired of hearing his teachers mangle it. In addition, he dropped his middle name and took on the more memorable Night. According to his father, he chose that name in part because of his interest in the Native American ritual of telling stories around a campfire at night, and in part because it's only at night that a person can look out at the stars and glimpse the greater universe. There was a practical consideration, as well. As Shyamalan's father puts it, Night is "a good entertainment name."

○ A. Why did Shyamalan change his name to Night?
○ B. Why did Shyamalan like sitting near campfires?
○ C. Why did Shyamalan want to be an entertainer?

◆ **Suppose you couldn't answer the question you selected above. Write two fix-up strategies you might use to find the answer.**

2. ____

____

____

____

_____ Number of Correct Answers: Part B

C Using Words

◆ **Complete each sentence with a word from the box. Write the missing word on the line.**

mangle	**unveiling**	**unconventional**
psychologist	**inaction**	

1. The school's dress code did not allow any clothing that was too

_________________.

2. He wants to become a _________________ because he is curious about how the mind works.

3. The highlight of the day was the _________________ of the design for the new building.

4. The nervous actor spoke slowly so he wouldn't make a mistake and

_________________ his lines.

5. The soccer goalie's _________________ almost caused her team to lose the game.

◆ **Choose one word from the box. Write a sentence using the word.**

6. word: _________________

____

_____ Number of Correct Answers: Part C

D Writing About It

Write a Movie Review

◆ Write a movie review of The Sixth Sense. Include information about what type of movie it is, what it's about, who directs it, and what actors star in it. Write at least four sentences. Use the checklist on page 103 to check your work.

____

____

____

____

____

____

____

____

____

Lesson 4 Add your correct answers from parts A, B, and C to get your total score. Then find the percentage for your total score on the chart below. Record your percentage on the graph on page 105.

______ Total Score for Parts A, B, and C

______ Percentage

Total Score	1	2	3	4	5	6	7	8	9	10	11	12	13
Percentage	8	15	23	31	38	46	54	62	69	77	85	92	100

Tom Brady

Surprise Superstar

Birth Name Thomas Edward Patrick Brady Jr.

Birth Date and Place August 3, 1977, San Mateo, California

Home Boston, Massachusetts

Think About What You Know

Was there ever a time when you did something very well even though others questioned your ability? Read the article and find out about Tom Brady's surprising performance in the 2002 Super Bowl.

Word Power

What do the words below tell you about the article?

obscure not well known

completions in football, forward passes that are successfully caught

recruit a new member of a group or team

diligently with careful and continuous attention

designating selecting for a particular purpose

Reading Skill

Fact and Opinion A **fact** is a statement that can be proved. A fact can be checked using a reference source. An **opinion** is someone's own idea or belief about something. When a statement includes words that show judgment, such as *best, most important, greatest,* or *should,* that statement usually contains someone's opinion. Adjectives that show judgment, such as *wonderful* or *amazing,* also show someone's opinion.

Example

Fact The first Super Bowl took place in 1967.

Opinion Today, football is the greatest team sport in the United States.

The statement "The first Super Bowl took place in 1967" is a fact that can be proved. The statement "Today, football is the greatest team sport in the United States" is an opinion because it expresses a judgment about football. What clue word in the second statement helps show the reader that it is an opinion?

Tom Brady

Surprise Superstar

When the New England Patriots arrived at the Louisiana Superdome for the 2002 Super Bowl, they were distinct underdogs. Most people thought the opposing team, the St. Louis Rams, would defeat them. The Rams were generally considered to have the most powerful offense in the league, led by experienced quarterback Kurt Warner, who had earned the title of Most Valuable Player in a previous Super Bowl. The Patriots, on the other hand, had an **obscure** young quarterback named Tom Brady. Most fans hadn't even heard of Brady. But Brady was to become one of the most celebrated players in the National Football League (NFL).

2 Brady's career had followed an unusual path. While the best quarterbacks frequently emerge as stars during their college years, Brady had remained in the shadows. He played well at the University of Michigan, even setting the school record for pass **completions** as a junior. But NFL scouts didn't think he would be successful in the pros. They didn't believe his arm was strong enough, and they didn't think he was fast enough on his feet. Brady's college coaches tended to agree. They saw more potential in Drew Henson, a player three years behind Brady. In fact, during Brady's senior year at Michigan, Brady had to share the job of quarterback with Henson.

3 When the NFL 2000 draft was conducted, Brady wasn't the number-one pick. He wasn't picked second or third—or even 103rd. It wasn't until the sixth round of the draft that the Patriots finally selected him, making him the 199th player chosen overall. Brady later admitted he was heartbroken to be selected so late. He knew that players who are drafted in the later rounds have little chance of becoming stars in the NFL.

4 When Brady began practicing with the Patriots, though, the coaches saw something they liked. Brady was smart, didn't wilt under pressure, and showed terrific leadership skills. Most NFL teams carry just three quarterbacks, and the Patriots already had three quarterbacks more experienced than Brady. But the Patriots were reluctant to cut this new **recruit,** so they kept him on as a fourth-string quarterback. That entire year he played in just one game, attempting three passes and completing one. "He was frustrated with his playing time," acknowledged teammate David Nugent, "but he'd say, 'It's not the coach's fault, it's not my teammates, it's me; I'm not working hard enough.'"

5 After the season ended, Brady went to the weight room and worked **diligently** to increase his strength. When he had first joined the Patriots, the 6-foot-4-inch Brady was rather skinny, weighing just 204 pounds. By the start of his second season, he weighed 220 pounds and was much stronger, and his passes had a lot more zip. The coaches were impressed enough to move Brady up in their rankings, **designating** him the second-string quarterback behind starter Drew Bledsoe.

6 Then, in the second game of that season, Drew Bledsoe went down with a serious injury, and suddenly Brady became the starting quarterback. With the team's record at 0 and 2 and Bledsoe out for weeks, most observers thought the Patriots were in the worst possible position to make the playoffs. But then something remarkable happened. Under Brady's leadership, the Patriots began to improve.

Skill Break

Fact and Opinion

Look at paragraph 6 on this page. The paragraph describes what happened after Drew Bledsoe was injured.

Which statement in this paragraph shows an **opinion?**

What **clue words** did you use?

7 Brady proved to be an exceptionally clever quarterback. He made some mistakes, but he learned from them. In game after game, he kept his teammates focused and his opponents confused. Although the Patriots lost a few games under Brady, they won more. Brady performed so well that even when Bledsoe recovered from his injury, Coach Bill Belichick kept Brady as the starting quarterback. The Patriots ended the regular season with an 11 and 5 record, securing them a spot in the playoffs.

8 In the first game of the playoffs, the Patriots beat the tough Oakland Raiders in overtime, 16 to 13, with Brady completing eight consecutive passes to set up the winning field goal. But in the next game, against the Pittsburgh Steelers, Brady twisted his ankle and had to leave the game. Drew Bledsoe replaced him and led the team to victory, 24 to 17. That meant the Patriots were going to the Super Bowl to challenge the St. Louis Rams—but who would be their starting quarterback?

9 With the championship on the line, many fans thought Drew Bledsoe was the best choice for the job, but Coach Belichick chose to stay with Brady. Although that choice made many New England fans nervous, Brady himself was calm and confident. In fact, on the afternoon of the game, he climbed onto the trainer's table and took a nap. And as the game progressed, the Patriots performed better than people had expected. With 81 seconds left to play, the game was tied 17 to 17. The Patriots had possession of the ball but were deep in their own territory, far from a touchdown or even a field goal. Everyone thought they would play cautiously until time ran out, thus forcing the game into overtime.

- Brady's favorite food is onion rings.
- He was a baseball star in high school.
- He loves to wear hats.
- He almost always stops to sign autographs for children.

Patriots quarterback Tom Brady winds up for a pass during a championship game against the Pittsburg Steelers.

10 Coach Belichick, however, had other ideas. He believed his young quarterback could lead the team to victory in the fourth quarter.

11 "Let's go for it," he said.

12 It was a high-risk decision. After all, Brady was only 24 years old and had never been in a situation like this before. What if he made a mistake, such as fumbling the ball or allowing the Rams to intercept one of his passes? Then the Rams would be in a great position to score and win the game. Belichick knew the dangers, but he felt certain Brady would rise to the challenge.

13 When Brady heard Belichick's plan, he looked surprised but unafraid. He went out and moved his team steadily down the field, getting the Patriots to the other team's 30-yard line in just seven plays. Then with 7 seconds left, Adam Vinatieri, the team's kicker, rushed onto the field and booted a 48-yard field goal to win the game and secure New England's very first Super Bowl title.

14 For his tremendous performance, Brady was voted Most Valuable Player (MVP) of the 2002 Super Bowl, making him the youngest quarterback ever to win this honor. He went on to lead the Patriots to additional Super Bowl victories in 2004 and 2005. Against all odds, the 199th pick in the 2000 draft has turned out to be one of the greatest quarterbacks of all time.

A Understanding What You Read

◆ **Fill in the circle next to the correct answer.**

1. At the University of Michigan, Brady

○ A. looked like a good choice for the NFL.
○ B. worked out to increase his strength.
○ C. set a record for pass completions.

2. What caused Patriots coaches to make Brady their second-string quarterback?

○ A. Brady became stronger and threw faster passes.
○ B. Drew Bledsoe had been performing poorly in games.
○ C. The fans and reporters insisted on seeing Brady play.

3. The decision of the Patriots to try to score in the last seconds of the 2002 Super Bowl was risky because

○ A. Drew Bledsoe had been injured by the Rams' defense.
○ B. Coach Belichick was not sure Brady could do the job.
○ C. the Rams could have intercepted the ball and scored.

4. In the 2002 Super Bowl, how was Tom Brady an example of a hero?

○ A. He was happy that he was asked to play.
○ B. He twisted his ankle in the playoffs.
○ C. He led the team to a winning field goal.

5. If you were a football talent scout, how would you use the information in the article to choose good players?

○ A. I would focus on players at the University of Michigan.
○ B. I would look carefully for players with hidden abilities.
○ C. I would choose only players who are good quarterbacks.

______ Number of Correct Answers: Part A

B Understanding Fact and Opinion

◆ **Read the paragraph below. Write the letter *O* on the lines next to the statements that show someone's opinion. Write the letter *F* on the lines next to the statements that are facts.**

1.

Brady's career had followed an unusual path. While the best quarterbacks frequently emerge as stars during their college years, Brady had remained in the shadows. He played well at the University of Michigan, even setting the school record for pass completions as a junior. But NFL scouts didn't think he would be successful in the pros. They didn't believe his arm was strong enough, and they didn't think he was fast enough on his feet. Brady's college coaches tended to agree. They saw more potential in Drew Henson, a player three years behind Brady. In fact, during Brady's senior year at Michigan, Brady had to share the job of quarterback with Henson.

______ Brady set the school record for pass completions as a junior.

______ NFL scouts didn't believe his arm was strong enough.

______ They didn't think he was fast enough on his feet.

______ Brady had to share the job of quarterback with Drew Henson.

◆ **Reread paragraph 9 from the article. Write one statement from the paragraph that shows someone's opinion. Then write the clue words from the statement.**

2. Opinion: ____

Clue words: ____

______ Number of Correct Answers: Part B

C Using Words

◆ The words and phrases in the list below relate to the words in the box. Some words or phrases in the list have a meaning that is the same as or similar to a word in the box. Some have the opposite meaning. Write the related word from the box on each line. Use each word from the box twice.

obscure	recruit	designating
completions	diligently	

Same or similar meaning

1. choosing ____________________
2. newcomer ____________________
3. catches ____________________
4. unusual ____________________
5. with care ____________________

Opposite meaning

6. quickly ____________________
7. familiar ____________________
8. missed passes ____________________
9. rejecting ____________________
10. veteran ____________________

______ Number of Correct Answers: Part C

D Writing About It

Write a News Article

◆ Suppose you had been a reporter covering the 2002 Super Bowl. Write a news story about Tom Brady's role in the Patriots' victory over the Rams. Write at least four sentences. Use the checklist on page 103 to check your work.

____

____

____

____

____

____

____

____

____

Lesson 5 Add your correct answers from parts A, B, and C to get your total score. Then find the percentage for your total score on the chart below. Record your percentage on the graph on page 105.

_____ Total Score for Parts A, B, and C

_____ Percentage

Total Score	1	2	3	4	5	6	7	8	9	10	11	12	13	14	15	16	17
Percentage	6	12	18	24	29	35	41	47	53	59	65	70	76	82	88	94	100

Chamique Holdsclaw

Focused on Basketball

Birth Name Chamique Shaunta Holdsclaw

Birth Date and Place August 9, 1977, Flushing, New York

Home Los Angeles, California

Think About What You Know

Do you have someone in your life who helps you focus and follow important rules? Read the article to find out how Chamique Holdsclaw became a star basketball player with help from her grandmother's rules.

Word Power

What do the words below tell you about the article?

overprotective protecting from harm to too great a degree

option an opportunity to choose

tuition the cost of classes at a school

curfew a rule requiring people to be home at a certain time

subsequent coming or occurring after

Reading Skill

Drawing Conclusions Good readers **draw conclusions.** They combine information from several parts of an article with what they already know to find a bigger idea. As you read, look for details in the text that provide clues about the people and events in the article. Then, when you draw a conclusion, make sure it is supported by at least two clues in the text.

Example

Women's basketball does not have nearly as many fans as men's basketball. And men's basketball has more television viewers. As a result, WNBA salaries are around $50,000 a year, while the men in the NBA make millions of dollars a year.

What do you already know about basketball? You might know *that male basketball players are usually more well-known than female players.* So a conclusion that you might draw from this paragraph is that *the salaries of basketball players depend on their popularity.* What are two clues from the paragraph that support this conclusion?

Chamique Holdsclaw

Focused on Basketball

There wasn't much that could keep her off the basketball courts. Any time of year, in any kind of weather, Chamique Holdsclaw was out dribbling, shooting, and rebounding. She practiced in the wind and the rain and the cold. She practiced in the heat of summer, playing six or even eight hours a day. For Holdsclaw, basketball was more than a sport: it was a passion.

2 Holdsclaw was born in Flushing, New York, the daughter of Bonita Holdsclaw and William Johnson. She spent her early years with her parents, but they separated when she was 11, and Chamique was sent to live with her grandmother, June Holdsclaw. Although Chamique loved her grandmother very much, this new living arrangement was not ideal. June Holdsclaw lived in a large housing complex called Astoria Houses. Astoria Houses was home to many good, honest families but also to drug dealers and gang members. Located in a tough part of New York City, it provided lots of opportunities for a young girl to go astray.

3 June Holdsclaw knew this, and she vowed to keep Chamique out of trouble. "She put a lot of restrictions on me," says Chamique. Every day Chamique had to do her homework immediately after school, and every Sunday she had to attend church. In her spare time, she was allowed to play basketball—but that didn't mean she could stay out late. "I set a time for her to be home," said her grandmother. "If we say we're going to have dinner at a certain time, she had to be there."

4 At first Chamique resented her grandmother's rules. "I hated it," she admits. "My grandma was **overprotective;** she wouldn't let me spend the night at other people's houses." A couple of times, Chamique challenged June Holdsclaw's rules. Once, near the end of seventh grade, Chamique decided to skip school. Assuming no one would miss her, she went directly to Astoria Park to shoot hoops. She

did the same thing the next day and the day after that. But on the third afternoon, June Holdsclaw showed up at school to walk her granddaughter home. When she learned that Chamique had not been to school, she was furious. "It never happened again," says Chamique.

5 On another occasion, Chamique slipped away from church to play some Sunday-morning basketball. Her grandmother caught her again. Chamique can still remember how angry her grandmother was, marching over to the courts to retrieve her. "She came out waving her shoe," Chamique recalls. Chamique was embarrassed in front of her friends, but she learned her lesson: she never again tried to skip church.

6 As time passed, Chamique came to appreciate the structure provided by her grandmother. Eventually Bonita Holdsclaw's life settled down, and Chamique had the **option** to go back and live with her, but she chose to stay with her grandmother. She understood that June Holdsclaw's rules were helping her move toward a brighter future.

7 Meanwhile Chamique's basketball skills were rapidly improving. The realities of playground basketball made her a tough competitor. There were usually too many players for the available number of courts, so after each game the losers had to sit down and wait for another turn. The only way to remain on the court was to keep winning, so that's what Chamique did. She developed a soft fall-away jump shot that no one could block, and she came up with a terrific spinning move near the basket that caught opponents by surprise. She became so good that she sometimes took a bus or the subway to another part of town, looking for players who could provide tougher competition.

Fun Facts

- Holdsclaw's college degree is in political science.
- She wrote a book about her life titled *My Story*.
- Her nickname is "Meek."
- She is the only person ever to be named New York City High School Player of the Year for three straight years.

8 When it came time for high school, June Holdsclaw realized Chamique would get a better education in a private school. June didn't have much money, but she worked as a hospital records clerk and took additional part-time employment to be able to pay the **tuition.** She admitted that it was a sacrifice, saying, "We lived on a budget." But, she added, "It was worth it."

9 Chamique enrolled in Christ the King High School, a private New York City school famous for its basketball program. There she established herself as a top player, leading her team to four straight state championships and an overall record of 106 wins and 4 losses. She also set the all-time school record for scoring and rebounding and was named an All-American.

10 By her senior year in high school, Chamique was one of the most highly sought-after players in the country. She had her pick of top college programs. June insisted that Chamique look for more than just a successful basketball program, however; she wanted Chamique to select a school with a solid academic reputation and an emphasis on team discipline. That school was the University of Tennessee. June was impressed by the coaches there, especially when they indicated that all their players had a **curfew** and that no one was a guaranteed starter. "Chamique," they warned, "you have to earn everything you get."

Skill Break

Draw Conclusions

Look at paragraph 8 on this page. The paragraph describes June Holdsclaw's decision to send Chamique to private school. One **conclusion** the reader might draw from this paragraph is that *June Holdsclaw believed that a good education is very important.*

How do the **clues** in the paragraph support this conclusion?

How does **what you already know** support this conclusion?

Chamique Holdsclaw drives the ball down the court during a WNBA game against her former team, the Washington Mystics.

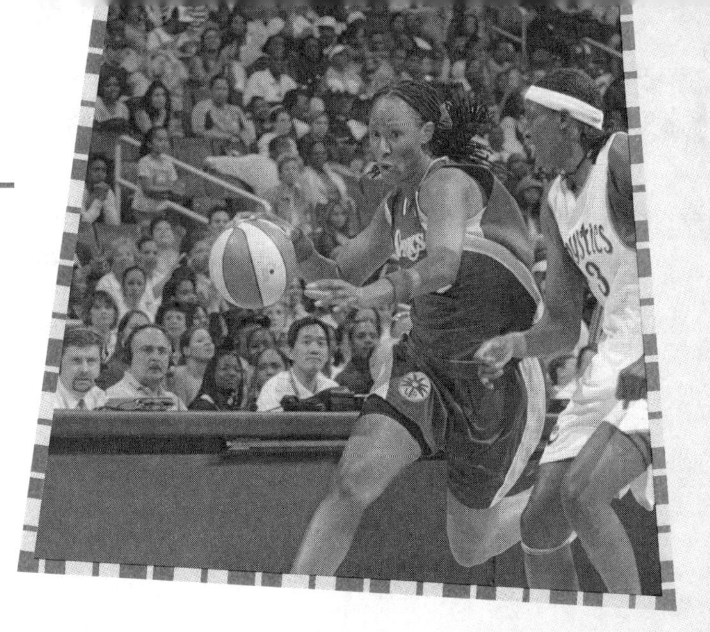

11 That was just what June Holdsclaw wanted to hear. "If you've got discipline," she declared, "that's all I need to know."

12 Chamique didn't disappoint her grandmother or her coaches at the University of Tennessee. She became the only first-year player in team history to start every game, leading the Lady Volunteers in both scoring and rebounding. Tennessee won the NCAA title that year, as well as the two **subsequent** years.

13 After graduation, Chamique entered the Women's National Basketball Association (WNBA), where she went to the Washington Mystics as the top pick in that year's WNBA draft. Chamique played for Washington for six years. Although the Mystics weren't a particularly strong team, she was named to the All-Star team three times. In 2005 she was traded to the Los Angeles Sparks.

14 For June Holdsclaw, who died in her sleep in 2002 at the age of 65, Chamique's basketball career was important, but it wasn't the most important thing. "We never talk about basketball," Chamique said in 1998. "She'll say, 'Have you been to church? Are you eating right?'" For Chamique Holdsclaw, the lessons her grandmother instilled in her—and the love her grandmother gave her—should serve her well, not just during her career but throughout her life.

A Understanding What You Read

◆ **Fill in the circle next to the correct answer for numbers 1, 3 and 5. Follow the directions shown for numbers 2 and 4.**

1. When Chamique skipped church to play basketball, her grandmother

○ A. made her go home and do her homework.

○ B. came after her and embarrassed her.

○ C. told her she couldn't play basketball anymore.

2. Choose from the letters below to correctly complete the following statement. Write the letters on the lines.

On the negative side, ______, but on the positive side, ______.

A. Chamique's grandmother wanted her to go to a good school

B. Chamique's grandmother helped her achieve her goals

C. Chamique resented her grandmother's rules

3. Chamique went to a private high school because it

○ A. had a strict curfew.

○ B. was closer to her home.

○ C. offered a good education.

4. In which paragraph did you find the information to answer question 3?

______

5. Which sentence **best** states the lesson about life that this article teaches?

○ A. Focus and discipline lead to success.

○ B. Truly great talent is hard to find.

○ C. Don't be afraid to try something new.

______ Number of Correct Answers: Part A

B Drawing Conclusions

◆ Read the paragraph below. Fill in the circle next to the conclusion that is **best** supported by the information in the paragraph.

1.

Meanwhile Chamique's basketball skills were rapidly improving. The realities of playground basketball made her a tough competitor. There were usually too many players for the available number of courts, so after each game the losers had to sit down and wait for another turn. The only way to remain on the court was to keep winning, so that's what Chamique did. She developed a soft fall-away jump shot that no one could block, and she came up with a terrific spinning move near the basket that caught opponents by surprise. She became so good that she sometimes took a bus or the subway to another part of town, looking for players who could provide tougher competition.

○ A. Chamique had a strong desire to improve her basketball skills.
○ B. Chamique rarely practiced on courts that were close to home.
○ C. Chamique learned her fall-away jump shot from other players.

◆ What clues from the paragraph support this conclusion? Write **two** clues. Then explain how what you already know helped you draw this conclusion.

2. Clue: ______________________________

Clue: ______________________________

What I Know: ______________________________

____

______ Number of Correct Answers: Part B

C Using Words

◆ **Complete the analogies below by writing a word from the box on each line. Remember that in an analogy, the last two words or phrases must be related in the same way that the first two are related.**

overprotective	**tuition**	**subsequent**
option	**curfew**	

1. restaurant : bill :: school : ________________

2. lawmaker : law :: guardian : ________________

3. quiet : silent :: choice : ________________

4. hungry : starving :: caring : ________________

5. before : previous :: later : ________________

◆ **Choose one word from the box. Write a sentence using the word.**

6. word: ________________

____

____

_____ Number of Correct Answers: Part C

D Writing About It

Write an Advertisement

◆ Suppose Chamique Holdsclaw was coming to your school to give a one-day basketball clinic. Write an advertisement for the clinic. Include information about Holdsclaw's skills and experience. Write at least four sentences. Use the checklist on page 103 to check your work.

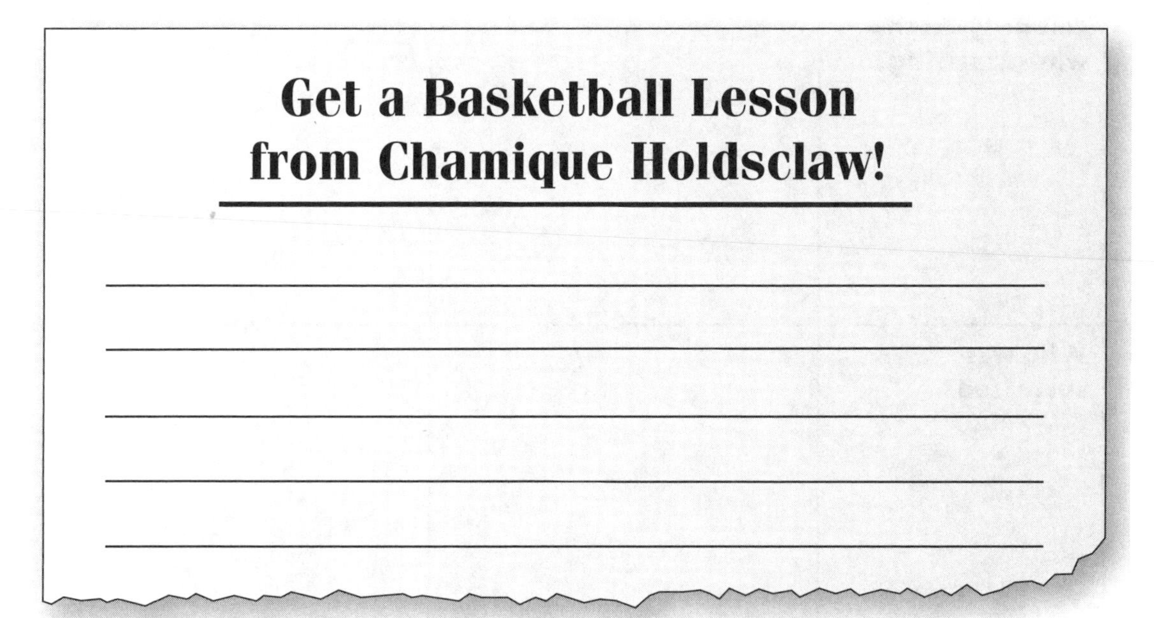

Lesson 6 Add your correct answers from parts A, B, and C to get your total score. Then find the percentage for your total score on the chart below. Record your percentage on the graph on page 105.

_____ Total Score for Parts A, B, and C

_____ Percentage

Total Score	1	2	3	4	5	6	7	8	9	10	11	12	13
Percentage	8	15	23	31	38	46	54	62	69	77	85	92	100

Compare and Contrast

◆ Think about the celebrities, or famous people, in Unit Two. Pick two articles that tell about a celebrity who did something surprising. Use information from the articles to fill in this chart.

Celebrity's Name		
What did the celebrity do that was surprising?		
Who was surprised?		
Why were they surprised?		

Unit 3

Jennifer Rodriguez

From Asphalt to Ice

Birth Name Jennifer Rodriguez

Birth Date and Place June 8, 1976, Miami, Florida

Home Park City, Utah

Think About What You Know

What is your favorite sport? Do you know if it's an Olympic sport? Read the article to find out why world-champion roller skater Jennifer Rodriguez decided to try ice skating.

Word Power

What do the words below tell you about the article?

gravitated was moved or pulled toward

trepidation fearful uncertainty

uncoordinated awkward or clumsy

insecurity lack of confidence

elite the best or most respected members of a group

Reading Skill

Asking Questions to Check Comprehension You can check your understanding as you read by asking yourself questions about the text. When you can't answer a question, think about what you might do as a fix-up strategy to help you find the answer. One thing you might do is reread the text. You could also ask your teacher or another student for help.

Example

In traditional speed skating on ice, two skaters race against each other on a 400-meter oval track. Each skater must stay in his or her own lane. In recent years, a new style called short track speed skating has become popular. In short track races there are no lanes, and four to six skaters race on a 111.12-meter oval track.

While reading this paragraph you might ask yourself, "What is the difference between traditional and short track speed skating?" One fix-up strategy you might use if you can't answer this question is to draw a two-column chart and label the columns "Traditional" and "Short Track." Then fill in the chart with details about each type of skating while you reread the paragraph. What other fix-up strategies might you use?

Jennifer Rodriguez

From Asphalt to Ice

It was an astonishing sight. Jennifer Rodriguez, the world-champion roller skater, was stumbling around the rink with her arms flailing helplessly. As she clung to the railing to keep from falling, a group of preschool children flew past her. While some observers may have found the situation humorous, Rodriguez herself was not laughing. Instead she was in deep concentration, trying to figure out how to make the transition from roller skating to ice skating.

2 Rodriguez grew up in Miami, Florida, where the only ice she saw came out of the kitchen freezer in the form of ice cubes. Her father had come to Miami from Cuba at the age of 13, and her mother had moved to Miami from Boston. Jennifer proved to be a natural athlete who quickly **gravitated** to roller skating and entered her first competitions when she was just five years old. Like many other athletes, she grew up dreaming of Olympic glory, even though she knew that roller skating wasn't an Olympic event. Her father also imagined Jennifer at the Olympics and often wondered aloud why she had picked roller skating as her favorite sport. Says Jennifer, "My dad was always saying: 'Why skating? Skating is not in the Olympics. Why don't you try cycling—cycling is in the Olympics.'"

3 Nonetheless, Rodriguez stayed with roller skating, and when in-line skates began to replace old-fashioned quad skates, she had no difficulty making the switch. As a teenager she became a top competitor, not only in speed roller skating but also in artistic roller skating, which involves making a whole variety of jumps and spins. She became so good that in 1992 she was named the U.S. Roller Skating Athlete of the Year. Between 1992 and 1995, Rodriguez won 11 gold medals as a speed roller skater in world competition, and she won a gold medal and several silver and bronze medals in the artistic branch of the sport. She is the only woman ever to medal at the World

Championships in both speed and artistic competitions in the same year. Remarkably, she accomplished all of this by the time she was 19 years old.

4 Soon after that, Rodriguez's career took an unusual turn. It happened after she began dating KC Boutiette, a long-time friend and fellow skater whom she eventually married. Boutiette had grown up roller skating but had then switched to ice skating. He had done this initially to improve his in-line technique, but he proved to be such a natural on the ice that after just three months he made the 1994 Olympic speed skating team. Boutiette encouraged Rodriguez to trade her in-line skates for ice skates. Although she was skeptical, Boutiette assured her that it wouldn't be much different. And so, with a fair amount of **trepidation,** Rodriguez left Miami in 1996, moving to West Allis, Wisconsin, where the top training center for U.S. speed skaters was located.

5 Unlike Boutiette, Rodriguez found the move to ice skating difficult and painfully embarrassing. As she puts it, "Here I was, a world class in-line skater, an artistic skater . . . and I get on the ice and can't do anything." For the first two weeks, she wobbled her way around the rink feeling terribly **uncoordinated.** "Being on a 16-inch blade was difficult, and ice is slippery compared to asphalt," she explains. "I would go home and cry because I couldn't do it. It's hard to be a beginner at something after being a world champion." At one point she called her parents in tears and told them she wanted to come home, but they convinced her to stick with it a little longer.

Skill Break

Asking Questions to Check Comprehension

Look at paragraph 5 on this page. The paragraph describes what happened when Rodriguez began to train on ice.

What **question** can you ask to help check your understanding of Rodriguez's experience?

What **fix-up strategy** could you use to help you answer your question?

6 Rodriguez also had a tough time adjusting to the cold weather in Wisconsin. Because she didn't own any warm clothing, she had to borrow winter gear from Boutiette. "In Miami, it's basically hot and hotter," she says. "My first winter in Wisconsin, well, it was very cold. Just walking from the car to the rink at 6:00 A.M. with the wind blowing in your face—I wasn't sure I could survive it."

7 With ongoing encouragement from Boutiette and her parents, Rodriguez kept plugging away, and at last she began to see improvement. She learned how to skate in a crouched position, how to take long, sweeping strides, and how to complete the turns with confidence. It wasn't the same as roller skating, but she could see the parallels. "It's not the same technique," she says, "but it is a similar motion, and you use similar muscles."

8 Once she mastered the form, Rodriguez made dazzling progress, becoming so fast on the ice that she won a spot on the 1998 U.S. Olympic speed skating team. Still, when she stepped out onto the ice in Nagano, Japan, for the Olympic competition, she felt a sudden **insecurity** about the whole endeavor. "I was hoping not to embarrass myself and my country," she admits.

9 Rodriguez needn't have worried. She finished a strong fourth in the 3,000-meter race. That performance placed her among the **elite** speed skaters in the world. She went on to win the U.S. and North American Championships in 1999–2000 and 2000–2001, breaking five U.S. speed records and earning the nickname "Miami Ice."

- Rodriguez likes snowboarding and playing paintball.
- One for her favorite books is *Lord of the Rings*.
- Her father made sure she grew up speaking English. Now she wishes she spoke Spanish, so she takes lessons.

Once a world-champion roller skater, Jennifer Rodriguez has become a top competitor on the ice.

10 When the 2002 Olympics rolled around, Rodriguez again made the U.S. team. In fact, she became the first American woman ever to make the Olympic team in all five speed skating events, from the relatively short 500-meter race to the much longer 5,000-meter competition.

11 Before the 2002 Games began, Rodriguez declared, "This time I want to win a medal, and I definitely have a chance." Her best hope lay with the 1,000-meter or 1,500-meter races. Although she slipped during one of her starts, she still managed to win bronze medals in both of these events. She thus became the first Hispanic woman ever to win a medal at the Winter Olympics.

12 Jennifer Rodriguez acknowledged that she had become an inspiration to other young Hispanic athletes. "It's important for me to be a role model for Hispanics," she said. "I've proved you can have the opportunity to compete in winter sports. Why not? Pick a sport you enjoy, and you never know what you might accomplish."

A Understanding What You Read

◆ **Fill in the circle next to the correct answer.**

1. Which of the following statements is an opinion rather than a fact?

○ A. It was an astonishing sight.
○ B. I was hoping not to embarrass myself.
○ C. Rodriguez was clinging to the rink's railing.

2. Rodriguez changed from roller skating to ice skating

○ A. after she competed in the Olympics.
○ B. after she began dating KC Boutiette.
○ C. when she was only five years old.

3. Rodriguez initially found ice skating difficult because

○ A. ice is slippery compared to asphalt.
○ B. she preferred artistic skating to speed skating.
○ C. her parents wanted her to try cycling.

4. From what the article told you about skating, you can conclude that

○ A. it's common to see Hispanic athletes in winter sports.
○ B. U.S. speed-skating records are broken every year.
○ C. there are more ice skaters in Wisconsin than in Florida.

5. The author probably wrote this article in order to

○ A. persuade the reader to find out more about ice skaters.
○ B. entertain the reader with a funny story about ice skating.
○ C. inform the reader about the career of a great skater.

______ Number of Correct Answers: Part A

B Asking Questions to Check Comprehension

◆ **Read the paragraphs below. Fill in the circle next to the question that would best help you check your understanding of the article.**

1.

Once she mastered the form, Rodriguez made dazzling progress, becoming so fast on the ice that she won a spot on the 1998 U.S. Olympic speed skating team. Still, when she stepped out onto the ice in Nagano, Japan, for the Olympic competition, she felt a sudden insecurity about the whole endeavor. “I was hoping not to embarrass myself and my country,” she admits.

Rodriguez needn’t have worried. She finished a strong fourth in the 3,000-meter race. That performance placed her among the elite speed skaters in the world. She went on to win the U.S. and North American Championships in 1999–2000 and 2000–2001, breaking five U.S. speed records and earning the nickname “Miami Ice.”

○ A. What place did Rodriguez get in the 3,000-meter race?
○ B. How many speed records did Rodriguez break?
○ C. Why did Rodriguez feel insecure at the 1998 Olympics?

◆ **Suppose you couldn’t answer the question you selected above. Write two fix-up strategies you might use to find the answer.**

2. ____

____

____

____

_____ Number of Correct Answers: Part B

C Using Words

◆ Cross out one of the four words in each row that does **not** relate to the word in dark type.

1. gravitated

tremble	pull	toward	attract

2. trepidation

dread	anxiety	uncertainty	attention

3. uncoordinated

crash	stumble	decide	struggle

4. insecurity

weakness	thoughtful	timid	afraid

5. elite

leader	privilege	gravity	exceptional

◆ Choose one of the words shown in dark type above. Write a sentence using the word.

6. word: ____________________

____

____

_____ Number of Correct Answers: Part C

D Writing About It

Write a Journal Entry

◆ Suppose you were an ice skater who trained at the ice rink in West Allis, Wisconsin at the same time as Jennifer Rodriguez. Write a journal entry describing what you might have learned about Rodriguez during that time. Write at least four sentences. Use the checklist on page 103 to check your work.

____

____

____

____

____

____

____

____

____

Lesson 7 Add your correct answers from parts A, B, and C to get your total score. Then find the percentage for your total score on the chart below. Record your percentage on the graph on page 105.

_____ Total Score for Parts A, B, and C

_____ Percentage

Total Score	1	2	3	4	5	6	7	8	9	10	11	12	13
Percentage	8	15	23	31	38	46	54	62	69	77	85	92	100

Jarome Iginla

The Future of Hockey

Birth Name Jarome Arthur-Leigh Adekunle Tig Junior Elvis Iginla

Birth Date and Place July 1, 1977, Edmonton, Alberta, Canada

Home Cranbrook, British Columbia, Canada

Think About What You Know

Have you ever watched a professional hockey game? Do you think hockey is a difficult sport? Read the article to find out how Jarome Iginla learned to master the game of hockey.

Word Power

What do the words below tell you about the article?

precedence a place of higher importance

honed made more effective or intense

uncanny being so far above what is normal as to seem superhuman

prestigious holding a high or honored position in people's minds

full-fledged having fully achieved a certain rank or status

Reading Skill

Fact and Opinion A **fact** is a statement that can be proved by checking a research source. An **opinion** is someone's own idea or belief about something. When a statement includes words that show judgment, such as *best, most,* or *should,* that statement usually contains someone's opinion. Adjectives that show judgment, such as *wonderful* or *amazing,* also indicate that a statement is an opinion.

Example

Fact Each year the Stanley Cup is awarded to the top team in the National Hockey League.

Opinion Hockey is the most important sport in Canada.

The statement "Each year the Stanley Cup is awarded to the top team in the National Hockey League" is a fact that can be proved. The statement "Hockey is the most important sport in Canada" shows a judgment about hockey in Canada, so it is an opinion. What clue words in the second statement show that it is an opinion?

Jarome Iginla

The Future of Hockey

He has been called "the future" of the National Hockey League (NHL), but no one would have predicted that when Jarome Iginla laced up his first pair of skates. Iginla, who was born and raised in Canada, initially found it difficult to get his bearings on the ice. Like many Canadians, he was introduced to hockey at an early age, playing informally at age six and joining a youth league at age eight. His first love was baseball, where he excelled in every position from pitcher to catcher to shortstop, but Canada's national winter sport is hockey, which often edges out other recreational activities. For Iginla, as for many young Canadians, hockey soon took **precedence** over baseball.

2 Iginla was rather clumsy on skates at first, so he spent his first two years in youth hockey as a goalie. But he had another good reason for choosing to play goalie: it was the same position that professional hockey player Grant Fuhr played. Iginla admired Fuhr's style, and he found it encouraging that Fuhr, who was African Canadian, had made it to the NHL. There weren't many African Canadian or African American hockey players—only 18 of them reached the NHL between 1958 and 1991—but Iginla was happy to know that there were a few, since he himself was of African descent.

3 After playing goalie for two years, Iginla concluded that there wasn't enough action in the net, so he **honed** his skating and shooting skills and became a forward. Even at this young age, he knew he wanted to be an NHL hockey player. "I never thought about the odds or chances of making it," he says. "That's just what I wanted to be."

4 When Iginla turned 16, he joined the Kamloops Blazers of the Western Hockey League. This league, which is part of Canada's junior hockey program, is a breeding ground for future NHL players. Iginla initially had a tough time adjusting to the fast and rough style of junior hockey, but within a year he got faster and rougher himself, developing a powerful shot and an **uncanny** ability to score goals. As he grew stronger, he began to win more battles in the corners and along the boards. Iginla also developed wonderful instincts on the ice, always seeming to be in the right place at the right time.

5 By the time Iginla was 18, he played right wing so well that the Dallas Stars of the National Hockey League drafted him. He never played for the Stars, however, because they quickly traded him to the Calgary Flames, who gave up their most popular player to get him. At the time, this trade was wildly unpopular with Flames fans. In fact, one Calgary newspaper headline read, "Jarome Who?"

6 In his rookie season with the Flames, Iginla established himself as one of the rising stars of the NHL, scoring 21 goals, accumulating 29 assists, and making the All-Rookie team. During this time, Iginla earned the affectionate nickname Iggy Pop. While music fans may recall the punk rocker who goes by this name, to hockey fans the *real* Iggy Pop is Iginla, whose stick has so much "pop."

7 Unfortunately the next year was a disappointing one for 20-year-old Iginla and his fans. Iginla struggled to find his groove and then broke a bone in his right hand, missing three weeks of play. By the end of the season, he had scored just 13 goals.

Fun Facts

- Iginla means "big tree" in Yoruba, a language of Nigeria.
- As a child, Iginla played piano and had a great singing voice.
- He is the first player of African descent to become the captain of an NHL team.

8 During the 1999–2000 season, Iginla experienced more ups and downs. He signed a new contract that paid him twice as much as before. But when he didn't get a single point in the first 11 games, fans grew angry. To some, Iginla was now Iggy Flop. Luckily, by the middle of the season, he recovered his form and once again led his team to numerous victories. Fans became so enthusiastic that they changed his nickname once more, this time calling him Iggy Top.

9 Then in 2001–2002, Iginla had his most impressive season yet, leading the NHL in goals as well as points and appearing in his first All-Star game. But perhaps his proudest moment came when he was named to Canada's 2002 Olympic hockey team. At the time, not many people knew about him. After all, he played in a small city on a team that kept missing the playoffs. During the Olympics, however, he was in the spotlight, with about half the television sets in Canada tuned in to see Team Canada defeat the United States and capture the gold medal. "I've never been more nervous or more excited than the Olympic final game," he says. "I'll remember that forever."

10 After the Olympics, Iginla continued to excel. In the 2003–2004 season the Flames finally reached the playoffs and nearly won the Stanley Cup, losing to Tampa Bay in the seventh game of the championship series. Iginla played brilliantly, scoring more goals—13 in all—than anyone else in post-season play. And that September he helped Canada win the **prestigious** World Cup of Hockey.

Skill Break

Fact and Opinion

Look at paragraph 9 on this page. The paragraph describes what happened to Iginla during the 2001–2002 season.

Which statements in the paragraph show someone's **opinion?**

What **clue words** did you use?

Jarome Iginla's impressive hockey skills give him and his fans a lot to smile about.

11 Today Iginla is a **full-fledged** star. But his skill on the ice is only part of the reason why fans love him. People are also impressed by his sunny personality and genuine goodness. He works hard, rarely complains, and goes out of his way to help others. He seldom refuses to sign an autograph and has been known to spend hours chatting with fans.

12 Once when his team was playing in Salt Lake City, Utah, he met some fans who had driven down from Calgary and were sleeping in their cars. Upon learning this, he found hotel rooms for them all—and then paid their hotel bill. Iginla has also donated time and money to many charities, including those for juvenile diabetes, spinal cord injuries, and cancer. In addition, every time he scores a goal, he gives $1,000 to KidSport, an organization that helps children from low-income families.

13 "People say he's too good to be true," comments Craig Button, former general manager of the Flames. "Well, it's true. He is that good." If Jarome Iginla is the future of the NHL, the league has a very bright future indeed.

A Understanding What You Read

◆ Fill in the circle next to the correct answer.

1. Iginla felt encouraged by Grant Fuhr's career because Fuhr

○ A. led the league in scoring.
○ B. was also African Canadian.
○ C. gave Iginla an autograph.

2. Iginla earned the nickname Iggy Top when he

○ A. led his team to many victories in 2000.
○ B. played right wing for the Dallas Stars.
○ C. broke a bone in his right hand as a rookie.

3. From what you read in the article, which of these is probably true?

○ A. Iginla has been one of steadiest performers in the NHL.
○ B. Iginla regrets the time he spent playing baseball as a child.
○ C. Iginla hopes for another chance to win the Stanley Cup.

4. How is Jarome Iginla an example of a good role model?

○ A. He works hard and helps others.
○ B. He belongs to a famous team.
○ C. He played in the Olympic Games.

5. Which sentence **best** states the main idea of the article?

○ A. Iginla joined his first hockey team at age eight.
○ B. Iginla is a great player in the National Hockey League.
○ C. Iginla is very successful at whatever he does.

_____ Number of Correct Answers: Part A

B Understanding Fact and Opinion

◆ **Read the paragraph below. Write the letter *O* on the lines next to the statements that show someone's opinion. Write the letter *F* on the lines next to the statements that are facts.**

1.

After the Olympics, Iginla continued to excel. In the 2003–2004 season, the Flames finally reached the playoffs and nearly won the Stanley Cup, losing to Tampa Bay in the seventh game of the championship series. Jarome Iginla played brilliantly, scoring more goals—13 in all—than anyone else in post-season play. And that September he helped Canada win the prestigious World Cup of Hockey.

______ The Flames finally reached the playoffs.

______ Jarome Iginla played brilliantly.

______ Iginla scored more goals than anyone else in post-season play.

______ He helped Canada win the prestigious World Cup of Hockey.

◆ **Reread paragraph 13 from the article. Write one statement from the paragraph that shows someone's opinion. Then write the clue words from the statement.**

2. Opinion: ____

____

Clue words: ____

______ Number of Correct Answers: Part B

C Using Words

◆ **Complete each sentence with a word from the box. Write the missing word on the line.**

precedence	**uncanny**	**full-fledged**
honed	**prestigious**	

1. He had an ________________ ability to predict the weather.

2. After she passes her flying test, she will be a ________________ pilot.

3. Her fashion designs won all of the most ________________ awards.

4. Finishing his homework took ________________ over playing computer games.

5. She ________________ her singing skills by practicing every day.

◆ **Choose one of the words from the box. Write a new sentence using the word.**

6. word: ________________

____

____

_____ Number of Correct Answers: Part C

D Writing About It

Write A Postcard

◆ Suppose you had been in Tampa to see the 2004 Stanley Cup Championship. Write a postcard to a friend back home about what it was like to see Iginla play. Write at least four sentences. Use the checklist on page 103 to check your work.

Dear ______________

____

____

____

____

____

____

Your friend,

____

____

456 Friend St.
Hometown, USA

Lesson 8 Add your correct answers from parts A, B, and C to get your total score. Then find the percentage for your total score on the chart below. Record your percentage on the graph on page 105.

_____ Total Score for Parts A, B, and C

_____ Percentage

Total Score	1	2	3	4	5	6	7	8	9	10	11	12	13
Percentage	8	15	23	31	38	46	54	62	69	77	85	92	100

Angelina Jolie

Finding Her Role

Birth Name Angelina Jolie Voight

Birth Date and Place June 4, 1975, Los Angeles, California

Homes Buckinghamshire, England, and Samlot District, Battambang Province, Cambodia

Think About What You Know

If you had millions of dollars, would you donate any of it? Read the article to find out about Angelina Jolie and her efforts to help people around the world.

Word Power

What do the words below tell you about the article?

eccentric peculiar or odd

vial a small glass bottle that holds liquids

insomnia an inability to fall asleep

media the different types of mass communication, including television, radio, magazines, and newspapers

genetically in a way that involves the passing of physical traits from parents to children

Reading Skill

Drawing Conclusions Good readers **draw conclusions.** They combine information from several parts of the article with what they already know to find a bigger idea. As you read, look for details in the text that provide clues about people and events in the article. Then, when you draw a conclusion, make sure it is supported by at least two clues in the text.

Example

Protecting refugees is the primary purpose of an agency called the United Nations High Commissioner for Refugees (UNHCR). A refugee is a person who has fled his or her home country due to fear of harm or persecution. The UNHCR strives to protect the right of all refugees to find a safe place to stay or live in another country.

What do you already know about people who have to leave their home quickly to avoid harm? You might know that *these people are in a dangerous situation.* So a conclusion that you might draw from this paragraph is that *refugees often have a difficult time finding safety after they leave their home country.* What are two clues from the paragraph that support this conclusion?

Angelina Jolie

Finding Her Role

Whatever she does and wherever she goes, film star Angelina Jolie has a knack for making headlines. Over the years she has cultivated an image as one of Hollywood's wildest personalities, with tendencies that many people would consider **eccentric.** During her three-year marriage to actor Billy Bob Thornton, for instance, she wore a **vial** of his blood around her neck. Then there are her tattoos—nearly a dozen in all, including an 8-by-12-inch tiger on her back.

2 Even as a child, Jolie pursued less common interests, assembling a collection of snakes and lizards with names such as Vladimir and Harry Dean Stanton. In high school she draped herself in black and dyed her hair purple. These adolescent years were not easy for her, and Jolie suffered from a range of problems including an eating disorder, **insomnia,** and depression. "I had a lot of sadness and distrust," she admits. "I've . . . had my times when I wasn't healthy."

3 Although Jolie's difficulties continued into early adulthood, she managed to build a career first as a model and then as an actress. In 1999, at age 24, she won an Oscar and a Golden Globe for her role as a disturbed girl in *Girl, Interrupted.* Jolie went on to appear in other hit movies such as *The Bone Collector* (1999), *Gone in 60 Seconds* (2000), and *Original Sin* (2001).

4 Jolie's biggest box office success came with *Lara Croft: Tomb Raider,* released in 2001. Much of this movie was filmed in Cambodia, an Asian nation ravaged by war during the 1970s and 1980s. Jolie's experience in Cambodia changed her life. The suffering of the Cambodian people touched her deeply. She was especially moved by the plight of the children, tens of thousands of whom had been orphaned when their parents stepped on land mines left over from the war.

5 Jolie wanted to do something to help, and so in 2001 she became a Goodwill Ambassador for the United Nations High Commissioner for Refugees (UNHCR). In this capacity she began making four or five trips a year to the most devastated countries in the world. Jolie goes to places such as Sierra Leone and Sri Lanka, countries torn apart by violence and civil war. Because she is a famous Hollywood star, the trips attract **media** attention and help raise the world's consciousness about conditions in these countries. Says one United Nations official, "Thanks to Angelina's involvement, UNHCR is now getting tons of inquires from young people wanting to help the cause."

6 Meanwhile, Jolie began to think about having a baby. This surprised her. "Growing up, I was never around babies or even small children," she says. "I'd never held a baby, except once in a film." Still, she couldn't deny her growing maternal impulse. Reflecting on all the orphaned children she saw in her travels, Jolie decided to adopt a baby. She said, "Somebody told me that if you're going to adopt an orphan, you should adopt from a country you love." For Jolie, that country was Cambodia. So in November 2001 she returned to Cambodia to become a mother.

7 "I went into an orphanage and decided I'd not go for the cutest child but just go to the one that connected to me," she says. As she toured the facility, a three-month-old baby awoke from a nap and smiled at her. She knew instantly that this was the baby she wanted. Adopting a Cambodian child is a complicated process, and it took Jolie four months to complete all the necessary steps. Finally she was able to bring the little boy, whom she named Maddox, home with her.

Fun Facts

- Jolie's father, Jon Voight, is also an Academy Award-winning actor.
- As a child, she was teased for wearing glasses, having braces, and being too skinny.
- The name Angelina Jolie means "pretty little angel."

8 Jolie didn't want Maddox to feel disconnected from his heritage, so she built a home in northern Cambodia where the two of them could reside for at least a portion of each year. Like other houses in the region, it is far from glamorous, consisting of three wooden huts on stilts with hammocks for beds and a hole in the ground as a bathroom. Adjacent to her plot of land, Jolie established a $5-million wildlife refuge that is home to tigers, elephants, monkeys, and other native creatures.

9 Jolie knows that she relieved Maddox from a life of certain poverty, but she recognizes that he has helped her as well. Having Maddox in her life has been a calming influence and has helped her deal with what she calls her darker emotions. "I've learned from experience that you can take charge of your darkest feelings and not let them destroy you," she says. She adds that, as a mother, "You learn to face up to your responsibilities. You stop thinking about yourself so much and stop whining about what's going wrong."

10 Jolie enjoys motherhood so much that in 2005 she adopted a second child, this time a little girl from Ethiopia whom she named Zahara. She says, "I'm drawn to kids that are already born. I believe I'm meant to find my children in the world someplace and not necessarily have them **genetically.** I like to think with every adoption I'm saving another child from an orphanage."

Skill Break

Draw Conclusions

Look at paragraph 8 on this page. The paragraph describes what Jolie did after she adopted Maddox. Two **important clues** in this paragraph are that *Jolie lives in Cambodia for part of the year* and that *her home there has a hole for a toilet and hammocks for beds.*

What **conclusion** can you draw about Jolie's character based on these clues? How did **what you already know** help you draw this conclusion?

While traveling as a United Nations Goodwill Ambassador, Angelina Jolie takes notes about what she sees at a refugee camp in Russia.

11 In the meantime, Jolie continues to fund several foundations designed to help needy children around the globe. These include the Maddox Relief Project in Cambodia and the Jolie Foundation for orphaned children in the African nation of Namibia. To honor her mother, who is part Iroquois, Jolie has also set up the All Tribes Foundation to help Native Americans. "I've given a lot of money," she says. But, as she acknowledges, "If you make $10 million, you can give away five and not miss it."

12 Jolie's work has earned her the admiration of everyone from relief workers to politicians to fellow celebrities. Former U.S. Secretary of State Colin Powell has said, "We are so thankful that there are beautiful souls like Angelina, people who so selflessly turn their compassion into action and not just words." Hollywood film star Brad Pitt agrees, saying, "Angelina donates staggering amounts of money."

13 Angelina Jolie may always have a wild side, and some people may shake their heads disapprovingly at the choices she made in the past. But no one can deny that she has made a difference in this world the way few other celebrities have.

A Understanding What You Read

◆ **Fill in the circle next to the correct answer.**

1. Jolie won an Oscar for her role in the film

○ A. *Girl, Interrupted.*

○ B. *Lara Croft: Tomb Raider.*

○ C. *The Bone Collector.*

2. What was the cause of Jolie's concern for orphaned children?

○ A. She made a movie about the Cambodian people.

○ B. She visited Cambodia and saw the suffering there.

○ C. She was asked to serve as a goodwill ambassador.

3. Jolie's house in Cambodia

○ A. cost $5 million dollars.

○ B. is next to an orphanage.

○ C. has hammocks for beds.

4. From the information in the article, you can predict that

○ A. many people will benefit from Jolie's actions.

○ B. other actors will begin to send money to Cambodia.

○ C. Jolie will stop acting and go to work for the UN full-time.

5. Which sentence **best** states the lesson about life that this article teaches?

○ A. Success only comes when you don't expect it.

○ B. It's possible to overcome a troubled past.

○ C. Most orphaned children quickly find new homes.

_____ Number of Correct Answers: Part A

B Drawing Conclusions

◆ **Read the paragraph below. Fill in the circle next to the conclusion that is best supported by the information in the paragraph.**

1.

Jolie wanted to do something to help, and so in 2001 she became a Goodwill Ambassador for the United Nations High Commissioner for Refugees (UNHCR). In this capacity she began making four or five trips a year to the most devastated countries in the world. Jolie goes to places such as Sierra Leone and Sri Lanka, countries torn apart by violence and civil war. Because she is a famous Hollywood star, the trips attract media attention and help raise the world's consciousness about conditions in these countries. Says one United Nations official, "Thanks to Angelina's involvement, UNHCR is now getting tons of inquires from young people wanting to help the cause."

○ A. The United Nations pays the cost of Jolie's trips to other countries.
○ B. The UNHCR is a stronger agency due to Jolie's involvement.
○ C. Most people have learned about Jolie's work by talking to their friends.

◆ **What clues from the paragraph support this conclusion? Write two clues. Then explain how what you already know helped you draw this conclusion.**

2. Clue: ____

Clue: ____

What I Know: ____

____

______ Number of Correct Answers: Part B

C Using Words

◆ Complete the analogies below by writing a word from the box on each line. Remember that in an analogy, the last two words must be related in the same way that the first two are related.

eccentric	insomnia	genetically
vial	media	

1. cereal : box :: potion : ________________

2. breathe : asthma :: sleep : ________________

3. congress : government :: newspaper : ________________

4. positioned : evenly :: related : ________________

5. expected : surprising :: ordinary : ________________

◆ Choose one word from the box. Write a sentence using the word.

6. word: ________________

____

____

_____ Number of Correct Answers: Part C

D Writing About It

Write a Story

◆ Think about how Angelina Jolie decided to become a mother. Write a story about Jolie's adoption of her son, Maddox. Write at least four sentences. Use the checklist on page 103 to check your work.

____

____

____

____

____

____

____

____

____

Lesson 9 Add your correct answers from parts A, B, and C to get your total score. Then find the percentage for your total score on the chart below. Record your percentage on the graph on page 105.

______ Total Score for Parts A, B, and C

______ Percentage

Total Score	1	2	3	4	5	6	7	8	9	10	11	12	13
Percentage	8	15	23	31	38	46	54	62	69	77	85	92	100

Compare and Contrast

◆ Think about the celebrities, or famous people, in Unit Three. Pick two articles that tell about a celebrity who made an important decision. Use information from the articles to fill in this chart.

Celebrity's Name		
What decision did the celebrity make?		
Why was the decision important?		
What was the result of the decision?		

Glossary

A

advocates people who publicly support a cause p. 26

B

bankrupt unable to pay off debts p. 14

C

celebrity someone who is well-known or famous p. 24

completions in football, forward passes that are successfully caught p. 46

curfew a rule requiring people to be home at a certain time p. 58

D

designating selecting for a particular purpose p. 47

devalue to lessen the worth or importance of something p. 27

diligently with careful and continuous attention p. 47

E

eccentric peculiar or odd p. 88

elite the best or most respected members of a group p. 70

executive a manager who leads a company or business p. 15

F

full-fledged having fully achieved a certain rank or status p. 81

G

genetically in a way that involves the passing of physical traits from parents to offspring p. 90

gravitated was moved or pulled toward p. 68

H

honed made more effective or intense p. 78

I

inaction stillness or lack of movement p. 38

insecurity lack of confidence p. 70

insomnia an inability to fall asleep p. 88

L

limousines large automobiles driven by hired drivers p. 4

M

mainstream following the most popular direction, activity, or interest p. 16

mangle to do something imperfectly or to mess something up p. 36

media the different types of mass communication, including television, radio, magazines, and newspapers p. 89

O

obnoxious extremely annoying and unpleasant p. 24

obscure not well known p. 46

option an opportunity to choose p. 57

overprotective protecting from harm to too great a degree p. 56

P

portrayal the act of playing the part of someone else p. 6

precedence a place of higher importance p. 78

prestigious holding a high or honored position in people's minds p. 80

privileged having a special advantage p. 4

prophecy something that was told or predicted beforehand p. 14

prosperity a state of wealth or success p. 27

psychologist someone who is trained in the study of the mind, emotions, and behavior p. 37

R

recruit a new member of a group or team p. 47

refined improved upon by removing weaknesses and adding finishing details p. 16

S

siblings someone's brothers or sisters p. 5

subsequent coming or occurring after p. 59

T

trepidation fearful uncertainty p. 69

tuition the cost of classes at a school p. 58

typecast to cast an actor repeatedly in the same kind of role p. 6

U

uncanny being so far above what is normal as to seem superhuman p. 79

unconventional out of the ordinary p. 39

uncoordinated awkward or clumsy p. 69

unveiling opening to view by taking away a covering p. 38

V

vial a small glass bottle that holds liquids p. 88

My Personal Dictionary

My Personal Dictionary

Writing Checklist

1. I followed the directions for writing.

2. My writing shows that I read and understood the article.

3. I started each sentence with a capital letter.

4. I put a punctuation mark at the end of each sentence.

5. My sentences all have a subject and a verb.

6. I capitalized proper nouns.

7. I read my writing aloud and listened for missing words.

8. I used a dictionary to check words that don't look right.

◆ **Use the chart below to check off the things on the list that you have done.**

✓	Lesson Numbers								
Checklist Numbers	**1**	**2**	**3**	**4**	**5**	**6**	**7**	**8**	**9**
1.									
2.									
3.									
4.									
5.									
6.									
7.									
8.									

Progress Check

You can take charge of your own progress. The Comprehension and Critical Thinking Progress Graph on the next page can help you. Use it to keep track of how you are doing as you work through the lessons in this book. Check the graph often with your teacher. What types of skills cause you trouble? Talk with your teacher about ways to work on these.

A sample Comprehension and Critical Thinking Progress Graph is shown below. The first three lessons have been filled in to show you how to use the graph.

Sample Comprehension and Critical Thinking Progress Graph

◆ **Directions:** Write your percentage score for each lesson in the box under the number of the lesson. Then put a small X on the line. The X goes above the number of the lesson and across from the score you earned. Chart your progress by drawing a line to connect the Xs.

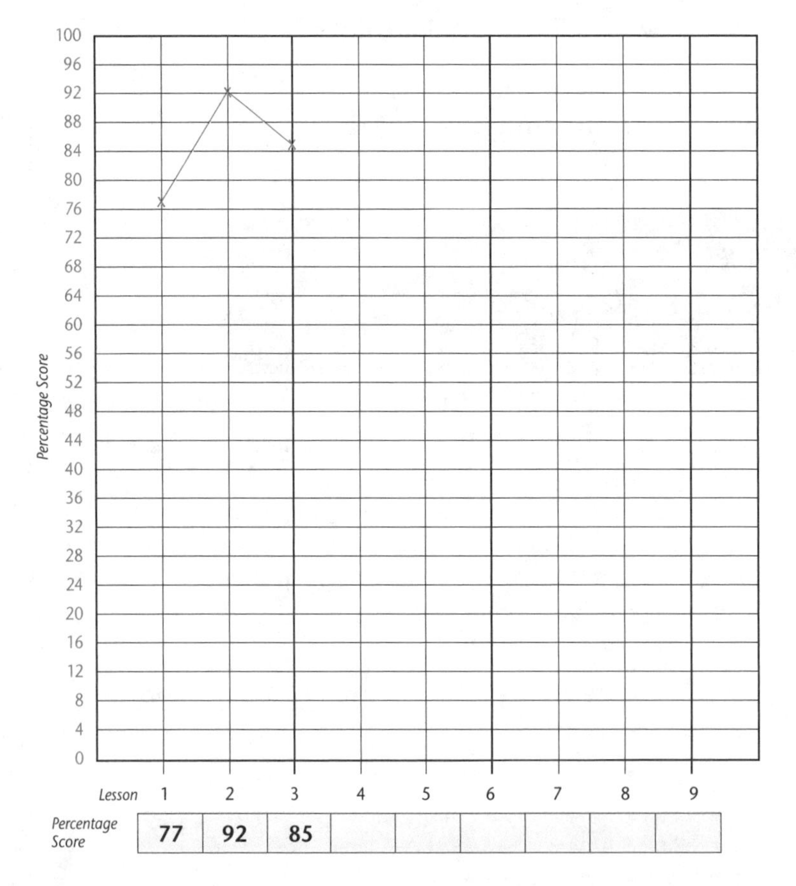

Comprehension and Critical Thinking Progress Graph

 **Directions:** Write your percentage score for each lesson in the box under the number of the lesson. Then put a small X on the line. The X goes above the number of the lesson and across from the score you earned. Chart your progress by drawing a line to connect the Xs.

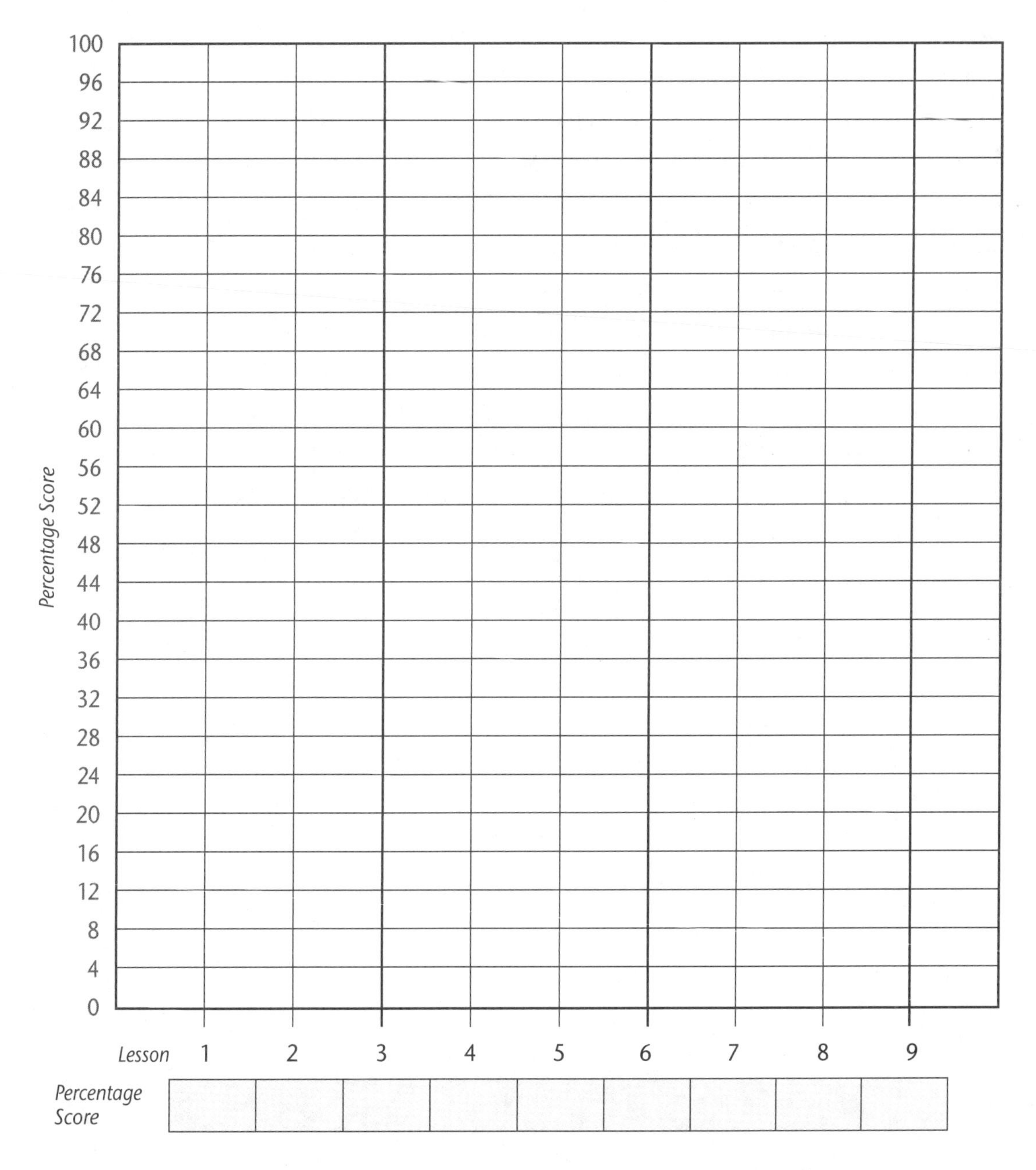

Photo Credits

Cover Carlo Allegri/Getty Images, (inset)Reuters/CORBIS; 1 (t)CORBIS SYGMA, (c)Reuters/CORBIS, (b)Brokaw Company/Getty Images; 2 Scott Nelson/AFP/Getty Images; 7 CORBIS SYGMA; 12 Juan Barreto/AFP/Getty Images; 17 Reuters/CORBIS; 22 Neal Preston/CORBIS; 27 Brokaw Company/Getty Images; 33 (t)Blinding Edge Pictures/ZUMA Press, (c)Mitchell Layton/NBAE via Getty Images, (b)Brian Bahr/Getty Images; 34 Carlos Alvarez/Getty Images; 39 Blinding Edge Pictures/ZUMA Press; 44 George Gojkovich/Getty Images; 49 Brian Bahr/Getty Images; 54 Nathaniel S. Butler/NBAE via Getty Images; 59 Mitchell Layton/NBAE via Getty Images; 65 (t)Douglas C. Pizac/AP/Wide World Photos, (c)J.P.Moszulski/AP/Wide World Photos, (b)Reuters/CORBIS; 66 Duomo/CORBIS; 71 Douglas C. Pizac/AP/Wide World Photos; 76 Frank Gunn/AP/Wide World Photos; 81 J.P.Moszulski/AP/Wide World Photos; 86 Matt Cardy/Getty Images; 91 Reuters/CORBIS.